AF471153

The Woman in the Corner

The
Woman in the Corner

GILBERT ODD

'Women are death on a crack fighter'
— George Bernard Shaw: *Cashel Byron's Profession*

London
PELHAM BOOKS

First published in Great Britain by Pelham Books Ltd
52 Bedford Square, London WC1
1978

ISBN 0 7207 1105 3

Set in Great Britain by Saildean Ltd, Kingston
in Plantin eleven on thirteen point
printed by Billing and Son, Guildford, London and Worcester

Contents

Illustrations

Referee Tommy Rawson helps Tommy Collins. 24 April
    1953
Collins, Tommy Collins Jr, and Mrs Collins

Lew Jenkins and Lou Ambers in the third contest for the
    world lightweight title. 10 May 1940
Katie Jenkins seconding Carmine Fatta in Brooklyn. 30
    June 1944

The end of the contest between Bold Bendigo and Tom
    Paddock. 5 June 1840
Rocky Graziano in his Brooklyn home, with wife Norma,
    mother-in-law, grandmother, and daughter Audrey

James J. Braddock, World Heavyweight Champion
    1935-7
Rocky Graziano moves in on Charlie Fusari

Mrs Luc van Dam and her husband. 24 January 1949
Joe Louis with wife Marva Trotter

Ingemar Johansson and family arrive in New York for his
    title fight with Floyd Patterson
Floyd Patterson down in the fight with Johansson

Jersey Joe Walcott, his wife Lydia, and their six children.
    5 December 1947
Sugar Ray Robinson *v.* Randolph Turpin. New York
    1951

Robinson
Edna Mae, Robinson's wife, at the fight with Jake
    LaMotta

Cassius Clay (Muhammad Ali) in his fight with Henry
    Cooper. 18 June 1963
Henry Cooper poses with twin brother Jim and mother
    Mrs Lily Cooper

ACKNOWLEDGEMENT

Photograph 7 appears by courtesy of Personality Pictures Inc.,
Brooklyn, New York

To
POLLY LAUDER TUNNEY
who had enough common-sense,
influence and money, to induce
her husband Gene Tunney to retire
undefeated as Heavyweight Champion
of the World and not to attempt a
come-back

Introduction

The women associated with any athlete must have an influence of some sort on his achievements, either knowingly or otherwise, and in particular when a totally individual sport like boxing is involved. In my many years of close contact with the profession I have been made aware of this on a number of occasions, right from the time when as an apprentice reporter at an amateur show I was startled when an irate mother belaboured with her rolled umbrella a referee who had had the temerity to disqualify her small son for an obvious breach of the rules.

More than once in my ringside seat, especially in the days when Chris Finnegan was fighting, my ears have been shattered by the screaming of loyal wives and girl friends, desperately anxious for their battling husbands and sweethearts to commit mayhem on the opposition. In the private homes of fighters I have heard the feminine reaction to their men's involvement in the Noble Art; usually and understandably, it is in an enquiring or even derogatory vein. It must be extremely difficult, I feel, for many women to appreciate why males should want to fight one another in the first place.

The sight of two well-developed men, equal in physical build, matching their fistic skill in earnest combat, is a heart-stirring experience for warm-blooded people of both sexes to enthuse over. But when there is a family tie or relationship between performer and watcher, the passion engendered is far greater. Many wives will not watch their husbands in action; others cannot stay away from the ringside. When Don Cockell was defending his British light-heavyweight title against Randolph Turpin at the White City in London, I saw Irene Cockell sitting at the ringside, for the first time so far as I could remember. As her husband was considered likely to be beaten, I was surprised to see her there and said so. 'I've come to see for myself,' she answered quietly. 'If Don gets beaten, he will come home and say it was nothing, then I won't mind him fighting again. But if I actually *see* what happens, I shall be far more satisfied about his future.' As it happens the referee stopped the bout in Turpin's favour, but Cockell continued boxing for several more years, even fighting for the world's heavyweight crown against the formidable Rocky Marciano.

Some wives take an active role in their husband's careers, even if it only amounts to attending to fan mail. Mothers may encourage sons in the early days of their boxing lives in a multitude of ways and then quite happily pass their duties over to a daughter-in-law when the time comes. Girl friends will sew initals on to fighting trunks and present colourful dressing-robes; the sister of Freddie Welsh, world lightweight champion and a vegetarian, always cooked her brother's meals in his training camp. In a previous book *The Fighting Blacksmith: the Story of Bob Fitzsimmons* I have told how Rose Fitzsimmons gave her husband the right kind of advice that enabled him to win the heavyweight championship of the world at Carson City, Nevada, while in another of my books (*Len Harvey: Prince of Boxers*) I have told how, in a behind-the-scenes manner, Florence Harvey was able to safeguard and further Len's interests throughout a long and highly successful boxing career.

On a certain Whit Monday, Freddie Mills' mother saw her son receive a black-eye whilst performing in a boxing booth in the West Country of England and remarked: 'Well, I've only myself to blame; I bought him his first set of gloves.' But she had done more than that. Her gift had inspired his keen determination to become a world champion. Joe Beckett told me that when he and his brother George were young men, their mother ran a travelling boxing academy; whenever business was slack she would call them to come out on the front and start a vigorous set-to that would draw in the customers. 'That's if you want any supper tonight,' she would add.

Frank Moody, one-time Welsh holder of the British middle and light-heavyweight titles, took his wife and two children with him on a prolonged trip to America in the 1920s. They travelled with a business manager and half a dozen other British boxers, and she cooked for the whole party, serving up the type of food that best suited them and making it unnecessary to depend on restaurant meals. Pierre Gandon, former middleweight champion of France, became a boxers' manager and ran a large gymnasium in Paris with the full-time co-operation of his wife. Madame Jannick Gandon not only looked after the personal belongings of the fighters when they stripped off for their training sessions, handed out the bandages and collected the subscriptions, but also was the only human timepiece I ever met. While the boys were working-out, she would sit in a corner of the gym and knit. When they were ready to start shadow-boxing, skipping, ball-punching and the like, she called 'time' and, at the end of three minutes, she called 'time' again. When the minute's rest was up, she once more called 'time'; there was no clock or watch in the place to guide her. She had been doing it so often that she could measure a three-minute round to a second and she never stopped knitting or ever dropped a stitch.

Tiberio Mitri had two ambitions in life – to marry a beauty queen and win a world title. He accomplished the first but it did not aid him in attempting to acquire the second. When, as European champion, he was given the opportunity to challenge Jake LaMotta for the world crown in New York, he took his beautiful girl-bride with him. He would have done better to have left her at home. At 17 Fulvia Franco had been crowned 'Miss Italy of 1948', and when they got to America, far more publicity limelight was thrown on her than on her husband. The Press photographers fell over themselves to have her pose for them, and poor Tiberio had difficulty in getting into the pictures at all. When she took her seat at the ringside she received a bigger cheer than that accorded to the challenger when he went into his corner for the biggest fight of his life; it was hardly surprising that he lost on points.

Jack Solomons made use of pretty girls when he matched Eric Boon to fight Jimmy Walsh, the reigning British champion, in his home-town of Chatteris in Cambridgeshire. Knowing that his young lightweight sensation had a host of girl friends, his manager sought them out and gave each a ringside seat. He had them sitting on all four sides. There was Babs from Bury St. Edmunds, Mavis from March, Pauline from Peterborough, Christine from Cambridge, the girl in the post office, the girl in the telephone exchange, the girl in the library, and so on. At the end of each round when Boon returned to his corner, Solomons would say: 'You've got to do better than that. Mavis is watching you.' Or, 'That was good, keep it up, Pauline is proud of you.' The result was that at the finish Eric had upset the odds by winning handsomely on points.

'Two-Ton' Tony Galento, the roly-poly New Jersey heavyweight, was on the point of giving up boxing after seven abortive years and a long run of defeats, when his girl friend caused him to change his mind. Mary Grasso pointed out that he got paid just the same whether he lost or won; that he loved fighting and she enjoyed watching him at work in the ring. 'If you quit now,' she said, 'we both lose something, so marry me and we will find a first-class manager.' They chose Joe Jacobs, who had gained fame by claiming a foul to give his fighter, Max Schmeling, the championship of the world. With Mary's avid encouragement and Joe's conniving they obtained a title fight for Tony with Joe Louis. That was a feat in itself because Galento was an odds-on favourite to lose. Yet he created a sensation by dropping the famed Brown Bomber in the third round before being himself knocked out in the next.

Sailors are reputed to have a wife in every port. Maxie Rosenbloom, one-time world light-heavyweight king, had a girl in every town in which he fought; more than one if it was a big town. And when I tell you he engaged in over three hundred fights scattered the length and breadth of the U.S.A., it will be appreciated that he never went short of feminine society. Nor could they have done him any harm, for in spite of being known as 'Slapsie Maxie' because he did not punch correctly, he remained champion for four-and-a-half years, and earned a million dollars, all of which he squandered on his love affairs. He received no encouragement from his mother. One morning his manager arrived with Maxie's purse of the night before. Ma Rosenbloom opened the door and eyed him suspiciously. 'I don't hold with my son boxing, so get the hell out of here.' Then she slammed the door in his face, but not before she had grabbed the slim sheaf of dollar bills from his hand. After that Maxie made sure he was paid in the dressing-room after each contest.

One Sunday morning in the mid-1920s a promoter called at a boxer's home in North London. One of his fighters for that afternoon's show was unable to appear and a substitute was badly needed. Getting no reply to his knocking, he enquired through the letter-box if there was anyone at home. A female voice from upstairs confirmed that there was, so he explained his dilemma but was informed there was nothing doing. They had been out late the night before and her husband was too tired to fight and needed a rest from the ring anyway. The promoter pleaded but in vain, then remarked artfully that it was a pity because he was prepared to pay more than usual and could go to as much as forty pounds for ten rounds. To his delight he then heard the wife order her lazy, good-for-nothing husband to get up at once as he was fighting in a few hours' time.

Perhaps the funniest story I know about fighters and their women concerns Kid McCoy, world welterweight champion in 1896. He claimed he had married ten times, one of his wives making two come-backs and then, to his great indignation, giving him grounds for a third divorce that was final as far as she was concerned. One day the Kid (real name Norman Selby) was fighting in Paris, and intrigued his opponent by continually glancing out into the audience. Curiosity finally overcame the Frenchman and he asked: 'Why is it that you are gazing into the gallery so much?' 'There's a beautiful girl up there who keeps giving me the eye,' responded McCoy; as soon as his opponent glanced to see for himself, he was promptly knocked cold by the Kid's celebrated left hook. In the dressing-room afterwards the defeated man complained that it was unsporting of McCoy to play such a trick, only to be told: 'Let that be a lesson to you. Never let a woman turn your head.'

Prior to World War I women were rarely seen among boxing audiences; in fact, they were barred from attending at places of respectability, such as the famous National Sporting Club in London's Covent Garden, although it was rumoured that Marie Lloyd, the music-hall star, was once smuggled in there dressed in male attire. It was left to such celebrated boxers as Bombardier Billy Wells and Georges Carpentier to attract feminine onlookers in a big way; the tall, blond, blue-eyed British Soldier because one never knew what might happen when he was boxing; the classical-featured, debonair Frenchman, because of his propensity for knocking out his opponents with a single right-hand punch.

Once women had acquired a taste for the Fight Game, it encouraged commercial promoters to organise big shows at large arenas and consequently secure the services of the best boxers by being able to offer large purses. Without the interest displayed by the fair sex it is unlikely that promoter Tex Rickard would have been able to stage his historic Million Dollar Gates, while the televising of important contests would be far less lucrative to its organisers if wives switched off boxing programmes in favour of something less masculine in appeal.

All fighting men are associated with women at some time in their boxing lives. For this book I have selected some of the more outstanding examples where the female influence has had striking effect, both good and bad, on famous characters of the ring. I have tried to tell my stories in the friendliest manner because all the women I have met in my long connection with the sport have been likeable and lovely people, equally enjoyable to meet as have been their fighting menfolk.

GILBERT ODD
Northiam, 1978

1

His Wife
Cost Him his Title

Jack Dempsey

One woman in particular influenced the fighting life of Jack Dempsey: Estelle Taylor, a young film actress. She entered his orbit when he was at the height of his success and their three years together terminated in his decline and fall. Not that Miss Taylor was to blame in any way. She did nothing deliberately to bring about his eventual defeat. All she did was to marry him, and there were many women who would have liked the opportunity to link their lives with the most sensational heavyweight champion of the day.

It was the eternal triangle that caused the trouble. Not that Jack was lured away by another woman, or his wife by another man. The third party was Jack 'Doc' Kearns, his sharp-witted and jealous manager. The 'Doc', so named because of his reputation as a masterly repairer of fistic facial wounds and who always carried his corner impedimenta in a small black bag, had a half interest in whatever his boxer did and resented bitterly the intrusion of a third person. He wanted no share of Miss Taylor personally; it was her influence that upset his applecart.

In the autumn of 1923, a month after Dempsey's twenty-eighth birthday, he was sitting on the corner of the desk in his manager's New York office, fingering a cheque that Doc had just made out to him. Ten days earlier Jack had knocked out Luis Firpo, the Argentine giant, in two rounds at the New York Polo Grounds, and now he was picking up his pay for his fifth title defence; a quarter of a million dollars (£50,000 in those days) for 3 min. 57 sec. of fighting. It was less than half the amount that promoter Tex Rickard had given Doc, but

Dempsey was satisfied. Kearns had brought him from a hundred-dollar fighter to world's champion in less than five years. He had steered Dempsey into earning over a million dollars in championship fights alone. From the life of a hungry labourer in a copper mine, Jack had come a long, long way, to live in luxury. It had been worth it to give Kearns a split down the middle of every cent he had been paid since they teamed up.

When the boxer asked what plans his manager had for the future, he was assured there was plenty to keep him occupied. Doc, who was extremely energetic when it came to keeping other people busy, told him he had arranged some appearance tours that would occupy Jack's time for the next three months until Kearns had worked up sufficient ballyhoo for another remunerative title defence. This, he planned, would be against coloured Harry Wills, who had been challenging the champion for a long time. It would be staged in New York in June, and in September there would be a title fight with Gene Tunney. From the two bouts they should gross a million dollars.

Dempsey was delighted at this information, but meanwhile he thought he would go up into the woods and do some hunting. He knew it was Kearns' keen brains as much as his own dynamic fists that had made their partnership such a success. He could leave everything in Doc's capable hands and take a well-earned vacation. To his surprise, however, he was told he could forget the hunting trip for a while. Mervyne LeRoy, a Hollywood producer, wanted to make a boxing serial with Dempsey as the hero. If it proved any good it could run for ever.

So Dempsey went to filmland where they made a picture called *Daredevil Jack*, then another named *Fight and Win*. Jack was passably good, so they thought up a full-length movie called *Manhattan Madness* and starred him with Estelle Taylor, at that time an ambitious young actress. She was beautiful and Dempsey fell for her. The film-making flung them together every working day on the set. In the evenings and at week-ends they were inseparable. The gossip writers noted the growing companionship. The news reached the Doc's ears and he was thunderstruck. He caught the next train to Los Angeles.

Always direct, Kearns gave his boxer a stern lecture, pointing out that fighters and women do not mix. Dempsey still had a few years of fighting in him and if he got serious with this actress, she would ruin him. When he quit fighting he could run a harem if he liked, but right now women were poison to a world heavyweight champion. He reminded Dempsey they had made a pile by sticking together with no one else interfering and that they were all set to make another million. He was ordered to give up the actress immediately. Dempsey said he could not do that. He loved this girl and she loved him and they planned to get married. He was reminded that he had gone through one disastrous marriage and was warned that this one could go the same way. (Dempsey had married Maxine Cates, a piano player, at Salt Lake City in 1916. They were divorced two years later.)

Jack begged his manager to meet her; that she was different from the usual run of girls who chased after boxers. Doc agreed. If he could not talk Dempsey out of the situation, at least he could warn the woman off. When Kearns met Miss Taylor he wasn't impressed by her beauty. He was rude, she was cold, and when he told her that she was not going to be allowed to come between him and his fighter, she replied coolly that neither would he be permitted to come between Jack and herself. 'If you want to continue as his manager, keep out of my sight,' he was told. Kearns muttered: 'We'll see,' and went back to New York. Then he did all he could to break up the friendship. He tried to get Dempsey away from Hollywood with engagements in other cities; refereeing, prize-giving, music-hall engagements, etc., but the film people held the champion to his contract and Kearns had to wait until the movie had been made. Jack was in no hurry to leave filmland. He was enjoying himself playing hero to Miss Taylor.

When Hollywood had finished with Dempsey, over a year had elapsed. Then Miss Taylor played her trump card. She took Jack off to San Diego and married him. There couldn't have been more than fifty guests; the majority of them were reporters and photographers, since Estelle fancied that plenty of publicity was good for them both. Kearns didn't come – he wasn't asked, and he tore his newspaper to pieces when he saw the pictures of the wedding.

He thought he knew one sure way of getting Jack back into the fold. He would get him a fight. He pressed Rickard to stage the match with Wills (the outstanding contender, in the opinion of the fight fans), but Tex was not willing. He and his political backers in New York were scared of the outcome of a mixed match for the heavyweight championship; they feared race riots, as had been the case when Jack Johnson defeated Jim Jeffries in 1910. Moreover, Rickard could see a split coming between Kearns and his fighter and he favoured doing business direct with Dempsey when Jack had spent all his available cash on Estelle.

Kearns had the same idea. As soon as Jack was broke he would come back asking for a fight. Well, all right. The Doc curbed his annoyance and waited for the prodigal's return. He had to wait a long time. Dempsey and his wife went off to Europe for a long holiday. Under her prompting Jack discovered he could keep himself in spending money without the aid of Kearns, also it came to him one hundred per cent. Estelle pointed out that as world champion he no longer needed any loud-mouthed ballyhoo. Promoters would come to him. And they did.

When eventually they got home from their prolonged honeymoon, Estelle astonished Jack by telling him she wanted to appear on Broadway in a play. It was *The Big Fight*, to be produced by Sam Harris and directed by the great David Belasco and was the fulfilment of her dreams; the only snag was that Jack had to be leading man at a thousand dollars a week, while Miss Taylor's salary was a mere three hundred.

The show was a flop. Dempsey couldn't act at all, and his wife's talent was limited. They put it out on the road, but it only lasted six weeks. Miss Taylor was annoyed at her brief role as a Broadway star where something more than her rare beauty was required. Everyone looks round for someone to blame for their failures and Jack was the nearest target. She explained to him that being married to a prize fighter hurt her socially and therefore damaged her career. Things reached a climax one night at the exclusive Club Richman. The Dempseys were there with a party of friends and Abe Lyman, the band leader, came over to the table and in the course of conversation, asked Estelle how her show business was going. She told him things were quiet. He suggested that she should bill herself as Mrs Jack Dempsey instead of Estelle Taylor.

That hurt. The actress liked to feel that her own screen and stage reputation had been founded on merit rather than through the accident of marriage to a world sporting celebrity. She considered that her own name was sufficient at the box-office. Lyman reminded her that her husband had drawn over a million and three-quarters against Carpentier; a quarter-million against Gibbons and over half a million against Firpo. He was box-office magic.

Estelle bit her lip. That night she asked Jack how he had spent so much money in the last three years? According to what she had been told he must have received over two-and-a-half million dollars from his last three contests. Yet, when they had reckoned up his assets recently they were so low Dempsey had thought it was about time he had another fight.

'Well, honey,' said Jack, 'you've got to remember that although I earned all that money, it was only on paper. There were expenses and taxes, the training camp cost plenty, besides the Doc and me always split it right down the middle. It is a fifty-fifty arrangement, it has been like that all along.'

Estelle was astounded. 'Do you mean to tell me that while you did all the fighting, all he did was to shoot his mouth off. You took the risks, he took the money. How do you know you even got half? Did he give you a statement after each fight? I'll bet he didn't.' Jack said that he trusted the Doc, but his wife declared that no one could trust a man like Kearns. She had summed him up the first day she had met him. She urged him that from now on he would do his business direct with Tex Rickard in whom she had every confidence. 'He's a gentleman and I like his wife. From now on every dollar you earn will be a dollar.'

At Estelle's prompting, Jack saw Kearns and asked him a few questions. What had happened to the movie money from his last contest and a few other things that had worried him in the past but which he had not got round to querying. It was a painful interview. Up to that point the Doc had taken half of everything, films, theatre engagements, circuses, public appearances; whatever was published under Dempsey's name and for which he was paid, even the return from real estate investments. It was a loose arrangement with no signed contract. Jack had been prepared to leave everything to his manager without question. 'Here's your end, Kid,' Kearns had told him from the start when it came to settling up after a contest.

When they first went into partnership Dempsey had been grateful for these terms. His share was becoming as much as five hundred dollars, eight hundred dollars, gold-mine stuff for a former pick-and-shovel man. It never occurred to him to ask what the gross or the net of a fight had been. But as the contests got more important, his reputation grew and the purses became larger, the newspapers began to print the financial details, sometimes even the amount Dempsey was supposed to have drawn. Jack would take out a pencil and divide that sum in half, but what Kearns had given him was a lot short of what he thought he should get. When he questioned his share of his earnings, he had been curtly informed that it was due to expenses and he had accepted this explanation without argument.

Now Estelle had awakened fresh doubts. Jack went round to Universal Pictures where he thought he had some money to draw. But there was nothing owing, his manager had picked it up, the cashier told Jack. Half of it had belonged to Kearns because of their arrangement, although he hadn't lifted a finger or even watched the movie. Dempsey went to see his manager and asked what had happened to his share. They had a bitter quarrel and to finish it Jack told the Doc he was through. 'I don't want to see you again or have anything more to do with you. If you want to stick around as my manager, it will be on a straight one-third cut, but that's all. We're finished in every other way.'

'I'll be what I've always been with you, or nothing,' Doc answered with sinister coldness. 'Good,' replied Jack, 'you're now nothing.'

'It may be the end, but it's not the finish,' Kearns told him. And when Dempsey eventually signed for his next title defence, the Doc started a series of law suits that lasted for years.

Estelle and Jack went to see Rickard. The big promoter had waited patiently for this moment. Dempsey told him of the split with Kearns and asked Tex to get him a fight and take over his business. Rickard told him that he was not in a position to do that, but he would put Dempsey in touch with a man who would take his legal commission and no more, and render an account for all Jack earned.

'Who have you in mind to fight me for the championship?' asked the fighter. Tex replied: 'I'm putting you in with Tunney, but not in New York. The Commissioners here are trying to force you into meeting Wills, but I don't want that match for several reasons. So I'm taking you and Gene into Philadelphia. We shall touch two million this time.'

Estelle should have been pleased at the prospect, but she wasn't. With the announcement of the fight all the limelight was thrown on her husband. She was, indeed, nothing more than Mrs Jack Dempsey. No one wanted her in films or in a play unless he was there, and now he was away in training – a long and necessary spell of conditioning in view of his three-year layoff and the soft living he had been enjoying since their marriage.

Kindly but firmly she had broken him in. He wore silk underwear now, fine suits and knew how to behave at table. They had lived in the best hotels in fabulous party style and luxurious ease of the Roaring Twenties. It was the way Estelle wanted to live and although never really at home in it, Jack enjoyed himself. He had been happy enough in his rough, uncouth way of living, now he was fast forgetting how to be tough. The cold fighting fury was still in him, but no longer so close to the surface.

As soon as Jack had departed for the training camp, Kearns

started a civil war against his former fighter. He issued writs that attached himself to everything Jack owned and was likely to earn. He produced a contract that Dempsey had been foolish enough to sign just before the Firpo fight, in which Kearns was entitled to a third of everything Jack was paid as a professional boxer. It had been necessary to have this paper to satisfy the New York State Boxing Commissioners before they would sanction that particular contest. It had been concocted to disguise the fact that in actuality Kearns took fifty per cent of Dempsey's earnings. Now the Doc used it as a legal document to get more money out of the champion without being his manager.

Kearns' biggest claim was for a third of a million dollars he maintained Dempsey would have received for the Wills and Tunney fights he had planned. Jack had no peace. He had writs delivered through the post, they were handed to him in the streets. His bank accounts were sealed off, people who owed him money refused to pay because they too were threatened with writs if they did.

The whole thing worried Jack to distraction and sickened his wife. The climax for Estelle came the day she was stopped on the highway and the car she was driving taken away from her on a writ of attachment. The adverse publicity she received made her furious, not only with Kearns, but with her husband. She told Jack she wouldn't come to Philadelphia to see him fight Tunney.

Jack became as nervous as a cat. He developed dermatalgia, a disease of the nerves in which the skin dries and cracks open. He had inflamation of the intestines, a pre-fight complaint that some fighters get but which Dempsey had never previously known. He wasn't fit to defend his title against Tunney. He wasn't fit to fight anyone as a result of his troubles with Kearns and Estelle. Tex Rickard came to see him at his camp and they had a long talk about postponing the contest. They came to the conclusion that it would not help matters if they did. It would not settle Kearns, it would not make Jack's wife any happier, and 140,000 fans were going to be disappointed. Rickard had such faith in Dempsey that he told him he could beat the light-punching Tunney even if he was only half a man.

So the fight went on and the turnstiles clicked to the then record figure of 1,895,723 dollars. Rickard had scheduled the bout for ten rounds only, in order to give Dempsey the best possible chance, but it rained throughout the contest and the ring-rusty champion slithered and slipped on the wet canvas as he tried to knock out his challenger, while Tunney, who had practised for weeks in running backwards, stuck out a straight left and cut Dempsey to ribbons as he ran into it.

The fiercer Jack fought, the more punishment he took. Tunney made him miss, hooked and uppercut him as he floundered past, stabbed him with the left and crossed him with the right. Only once, in the fourth round, did Dempsey look like winning. He remembered Doc Kearns' advice, 'Pull up your socks and slap the bum down', and charged into Gene like a tiger.

But not the old tiger. Life with Estelle had smoothed off his raw edges; the urge was there but the zip had gone. He caught Tunney with a right that would have knocked him cold three years earlier. Even then it was hard enough to make Gene sag at the knees and grasp the top rope with his right hand. But Dempsey's follow-up was so slow that Tunney had ample time to slip away and get on the move again, and he never gave Jack another such opportunity. At the end there was a new champion and Dempsey left the Sesquicentennial Stadium ring a broken-hearted man, his face a pathetic sight with both eyes closing and his lips mashed to a bleeding pulp. When he got back to New York, his wife greeted him with: 'I read the papers. What happened?' Dempsey then made the most historic remark of his life: 'Honey,' he told her, 'I forgot to duck.'

Estelle didn't even think it was funny. Now she was married to an ex-champion. Even when Rickard told them he planned a return match with Tunney in Chicago when Dempsey would be assured of another half-million dollars, she wasn't impressed. She decided to pick up her film career where she had left off.

They parted, and they got together again, but Miss Taylor's career problem was always between them. Because of her Jack had lost his manager and his title. Now he was to lose his wife. One day she left him a note saying she was going to Reno and Jack's misery was complete. It proved an expensive parting. He bought back, for 200,000 dollars, a house he had given her, and added another 100,000 to soothe her aches and pains. By that time Dempsey had gone through his second fight with Tunney and been beaten again. He was past thirty-two then; it was his last real fight.

Dempsey married Hannah Williams, actress in 1933. They had two daughters, but were divorced ten years later. In 1960 he married Deanna Piattelli, a business woman.

2

She had No Time for Losers

John C. Heenan

In these days when an American boxer can fly over here at a week's notice, having agreed to terms on the telephone, it is difficult to imagine the time it took to arrange an important international match over a hundred years ago. In 1858 prize fighting was in its infancy on the other side of the Atlantic, but fast becoming popular although, as in this country, it was regarded as an illegal form of sport and consequently was in constant conflict with the police.

This did not prevent the tougher youngsters of New York from doing battle with their fists and the first contest for the American heavyweight championship took place at Long Point in Canada between two rival gang leaders, John Morrissey and John Camel Heenan. Known as the 'Benecia Boy', because he had once been employed in a steamship company's workshops there, Heenan was a handsome young fellow of 23, with blue eyes, auburn hair and a heavy, drooping moustache. He stood 6ft 2in., weighed 13st. 9lb and was beautifully developed. Understandably, he was quite a ladies' man.

Although he knew how to box and was a good puncher, Heenan could not quite match up to Morrissey, who had his own interpretation of the rules, rough and ready as they were. For several rounds John C. put up a tremendous battle, but his rival proved too strong and by the eleventh meeting Heenan had barely the strength to come up to the line. He stood there swaying, whereupon Morrissey felled him for the full count with a mighty punch to the head.

Strangely enough, the loser gained the esteem of the public more than the winner. Heenan's game struggle brought him a lot of hero-worship and he was encouraged to challenge again for the championship. Morrissey was not interested, however. He had his heart set on becoming a politician and was, in fact, elected to the State Senate in 1877. There being no other worthy opponent to fight, the 'Benecia Boy' had to be content with an occasional exhibition bout, or wait until election time when he was invaluable as a strong-arm man.

In spite of his popularity, Heenan could barely make a living, and might easily have drifted into obscurity had he not encountered Adah Isaacs Menken. She was an ambitious young actress, with a beautiful face and a well-proportioned anatomy. She had left her husband, a musician in the orchestra of a touring company in which she played small parts, to come to New York. There she found fame in a role that suited both her physique and temperament. She also found Heenan.

Their admiration was mutual, and after a whirlwind court-ship they became married without bothering to find out if Mrs Menken was free to wed again. As the wife of a famous pugilist, Adah now secured plenty of vaudeville work, and was eventually cast in the classical part of Mazeppa. The producer gave one look at Adah and decided she would be a sensation. The play called for her to be strapped to the back of a horse that galloped across the stage, and for this escapade she was clad from neck to ankles in silk tights which not only accentuated her ample curves, but were artfully flesh coloured. This made it appear to the audience that, like Lady Godiva, she wasn't wearing a stitch. They called her 'The Naked Lady', and the public fell over themselves to see this 'naughty' play.

Heenan now bathed in Adah's limelight, as she had done in his when first coming to New York. He felt that his financial problems were over and proceeded to occupy his time in spending her earnings. Adah did not mind. She was working on a percentage of the takings, and averaged a thousand dollars (£200) a week, ten times more than a first-class actress could expect in those days. Besides, she was desperately in love with her Greek-god-like husband.

Then quite suddenly she grew tired of him. It dawned on her that being married to a common prize-fighter was more a liability than an asset. It interfered with her theatrical ambitions and she set about finding ways and means of getting rid of Heenan.

Tom Sayers, a Brighton bricklayer, was Champion of England and had offered to meet anyone in the world. Adah urged John to accept the challenge, proceed to England and give Sayers the licking of his life. 'He's only half your size,' she jeered. 'Go and prove that you are the best man in the world.'

She found friends to put up the money for her husband's passage and the necessary side-stake of £200. She used all the influence at her command to get the match arranged. John C. became so excited he went off without saying 'Goodbye'. His wife could not have cared less. Hardly before he reached Liverpool she had divorced him.

The fight between Heenan and Sayers, the first international boxing match of any importance, caused widespread interest throughout the world, despite the fact that it took over a year to mature. The police made every effort to stop it, even trying to get the American deported. They chased him from one training spot to another, until he pitched his camp at Trent Lock, on the borders of Derbyshire, Nottingham and Leicester, and so had the choice of three counties to cross into when danger threatened from the law.

Even these precautions did not save him from being arrested and placed on bail. He must have wondered if he would ever toe the line with Sayers. The English champion was also harassed by the law. He trained at Newmarket, and the day before the fight the roads were blocked and the railway stations guarded to prevent Sayers from reaching London. Eventually he travelled in a horse-box disguised as a stable-lad. A tremendous crowd had gathered at Shoreditch station to welcome his arrival, but Tom walked right through them unnoticed.

The secret site for the battle was a field outside Farnborough in Hampshire, and here they fought one of the greatest fights in the history of pugilism. It went 42 rounds and lasted two hours and twenty minutes, by which time the Englishman had broken his right arm, the American was almost blind, and the police had arrived to arrest them both. Wisely the referee called it a 'draw', and everyone bolted.

Naturally both sides claimed to have been in a winning position when the fight was terminated so abruptly, and when he got back to New York, Heenan found himself a national hero. But in gaining fame he had lost his beautiful wife. This hurt his pride as well as his pocket. He tried hard to get Adah to come back, but she refused.

Instead, she decided to take her sensational play to England. It opened at Astley's famous theatre in the Westminster Road, and was an instantaneous success. Of course, the prudes of the period raised their hands in horror. The actress was declared a brazen and depraved wanton. Yet the box-office did wonderful business, and Adah, who was a talented poet among her other accomplishments, mixed with such celebrities as Charles Swinburne, and Charles Dickens, who accepted the dedication of a book of her poems.

The same could not be said for her former husband. Heenan's popularity waned and he went to pieces with drink and dissipation. Then something happened to make him feel life was worth living again. Sayers had retired from the ring, and Tom King, former sailor in the British Navy, had become Champion of England. Hearing that Adah had divorced her third husband and was on the point of breaking with her fourth, Heenan decided to challenge King and, at the same time, endeavour to bring about a reconciliation with his former wife.

The fight with King aroused almost as much enthusiasm as that with Sayers. It took place in a meadow at Wadhurst in Sussex, and the American proved by far the stronger and heavier hitter. Time and again he put the Englishman down and in the 14th round poor Tom was knocked senseless. Heenan appeared to have won the day.

'It's all over,' thought the spectators as King lay unconscious on the trampled turf. But his seconds had other ideas. While one bit deeply into Tom's ear in an effort to revive him, the other complained to the referee that Heenan had been guilty of kicking. This caused a heated argument that took up considerable time, during which the ear-biting second had a brainwave. 'For God's sake, Tom, pull yourself together,' he shouted. 'Remember your poor old mother – £200 will save her from want.' As if in response, King opened his eyes and blinked. Soon he scrambled to his feet, and stood up to his confident opponent in the gamest fashion.

Ten rounds later Heenan had worn himself out trying to batter the Englishman into defeat. To the delight of the onlookers, King then landed a mighty punch to the chin, and John C. was speedily counted out.

If he expected any sympathy from Adah, he was doomed to disappointment. She might have listened to a conqureror, but she had no time for losers. Heenan implored her to re-marry him, but she was angling for bigger fish than a beaten pugilist.

Heenan returned to America and never fought again. He died at the age of 38 in Wyoming, a forgotten man. His wife went on to captivate Paris and other European capitals, until at the height of her fame she was suddenly taken desperately ill and died in her 33rd year.

3

He was
'Managed' by his Sister

King Levinsky

In most parts of the boxing world, blood relations are barred from the corners: dads, brothers and cousins are not permitted to act as seconds. It would have been to King Levinsky's advantage if his elder sister, Lena, had been refused admittance to any fight arena at which he was performing, for she caused him endless trouble and made short work of his fistic career.

It did not please Lena to know that her young brother was a professional fighter until she read in the paper that his opponent, Tuffy Griffiths, was getting 25,000 dollars for fighting the King at the Chicago Stadium. 'That's a lot of money for a few punches,' she thought. 'I must see him after the fight and get myself a loan.'

Levinsky, real name Harry Kracow, lived with his parents near the fish market. Lena was married, so visiting the old people was as good an excuse as any for making the touch.

Home came the King to toss a pile of dollar bills on the table and grin through his bruises. Proudly he informed the company that they amounted to four thousand dollars – which he didn't think bad money for beating his opponent, even if he hadn't received the verdict. His sister snorted. In the *Tribune* that morning she had read that the other guy had received twenty-five grand. If that was true, she wanted to know why he had not been given a like amount. It seemed strange to her that a man from Sioux City should earn far more than a home-town fighter. She knew that Harry was a local draw even if he was not a great boxer. He had won a lot of contests and must be worth more than a miserable four thousand bucks.

When she wanted to know why he had not been paid as

much as Griffiths, her brother told her, quite simply, that he was not worth it. He was a happy but simple soul; she was annoyed that he had been taken advantage of. She felt that he was in need of a manager. The King – he had given himself the name – assured her that he had Ray Alvis; he got the best money he could, which they split down the middle. The purse had been ten thousand dollars, but two thousand of this had been swallowed up in expenses, therefore what was on the table was his fair share.

Lena was not satisfied and the next day she went to the Boxing Commission's offices and applied for a managerial licence. With her overwhelming eloquence she got one without a great deal of argument, then she notified the King that he was now under her control. When he said that she knew nothing about boxing, his sister replied that neither did he. 'What you have got is a big punch and I am going to find the bums for you to practice it on. Between us we will make a lot of dough and it will stay in the family.'

Although she was not allowed to go into his corner, she sat on the ring steps and encouraged him with loud and fanatical screeching. Between the rounds she would jump on to the ring apron to bawl him out for not flattening his opponent and give him such garbled instructions that the poor King answered the next bell in a complete daze. She was up and down so much they called her 'Leaping Lena'.

No wonder he lost fights he should have won. But the results never bothered Lena. She screwed the last dollar from the promoters she bullied into using the King's services and her brother's purses grew with every fight. At the time when she took over his management, Levinsky had taken part in 48 bouts, won 36 and drawn three. In the next three years under his sister's direction he met 29 of her 'bums' and was beaten by 12 of them.

When someone criticised his record, Lena declared that whether or not her brother won was of least importance. What mattered was seeing that he got well paid for his services. If they took a look at his bank balance they would see that he was heading for his first million.

It was a good thing that the King was tough. He could take the big hitters his sister got for him one after another and absorb their best punches with a grin. No one stopped him until she put him in with Max Baer. The famed Livermore Larruper was world champion then, and they wanted Levinsky for an exhibition bout in Chicago. Lena got a fortune for the scheduled four rounds and her last words to her brother as he answered the starting bell were most sensible. 'Make a good showing tonight and I'll get you a re-match for the championship,' she promised.

Scared of not doing the right thing, the King misunderstood her completely. He went out from his corner in warlike mood, his right arm cocked for action. Baer had been spending his six months' reign as titleholder in the major night clubs. He could just about manage to get through the brief exhibition bout and no more. The last thing he expected was to face an all-out assault from what should have been a placid sparring-partner.

Whoosh! Over came the King's right swing and landed with a thud on the champion's wide grin. Max was knocked off balance, and before he could recover Levinsky had wound up another right and let it go. This crashed into the out-of-condition champion's midriff and made him gasp. Another right had Baer staggering and the fans yelling their heads off. For the first time in her life Lena was struck dumb. She dreaded to think of the consequences. Had her dumb-cluck of a brother gone mad?

Levinsky chased the champion all round the ring, trying to land a knockdown punch. Maxie, who loved the limelight, had to suffer the indignity of beating a hasty retreat. There was civil war in his corner when he got back there. The King was beaming when he returned to his sister and was astonished at the scowl he got. 'From now on I'm having no part of this fight,' she told him. 'You're on your own, brother.'

There was murder in Baer's eyes as he sat waiting for the second round to start, and as soon as he saw the timekeeper move to strike the gong, he darted across the ring and caught the unprepared King with a right-hander to the chin as he was in the act of rising from his stool. Levinsky was knocked cold;

he slid to the canvas and remained motionless while they counted him out. When he regained consciousness he wanted to know what had happened and when she told him he wouldn't believe it. He was not convinced until he saw the picture papers the next morning.

At the beginning of 1935, promoter Mike Jacobs was building up Joe Louis as a heavyweight threat, and was looking around for likely opponents who would not prove too dangerous. The assassination of Levinsky by Baer made him consider the King as a natural rival for the Brown Bomber in Chicago. He approached Lena, who turned it down flat. She told Uncle Mike that she did not want her brother to be finished just yet and that the beating from Baer had taken a lot of steam out of him. Jacobs advised her to take the King on a tour of the rural fight towns. After he knocked over a few mediocre boxers, he would come back full of pep and confidence.

Lena told him quite plainly that she did not intend building up Louis at her brother's expense until the artful promoter mentioned that he could afford to pay the King thirty grand. 'For that money we will fight anyone,' she answered. 'Where's the contract?'

At first Levinsky was overjoyed at the prospect of meeting Louis, but day by day, as he read the newspapers and realised that Joe was unbeaten and had scored 19 knockouts in 23 bouts, his enthusiasm ebbed away.

On the night of the fight, one of Jacobs' henchmen came to him at the ringside and told him that the King was paralysed with fear. He was so stiff with fright they could not get him undressed. There was an hour to go before the main event was due to be staged, but Jacobs was taking no chances. 'Get these two preliminary boys out of the ring and bring in Louis, I'll go and attend to Levinsky.' They almost had to carry the King to his corner, during the announcing he had to be held on to his stool. The starting bell sounded, Louis glided out and they gave Levinsky a shove to go forth and meet him.

It was a massacre that lasted 2 min. 21 sec.; in that short time Levinsky was flattened three times, and was sitting on the lower rope dumbly pleading for mercy when the referee called a halt. The King hadn't landed one blow in self-defence. He had back-pedalled round the ring until Louis tagged him with a powerful left hook that decked Levinsky the first time and started the rot.

They picked up the King and led him stumbling back to Lena. She knew it was the end, sold the King's contract, and went back to her knitting. Levinsky never again appeared in a Chicago ring. In less than two years he was a washed-up fighter, knocked out four times in his last seven fights, all of which he lost. Yet he never resented his sister's interference; in fact he told everyone that but for her he would have got nowhere. And his listeners smiled, for that is just about where she did get him. When he hung up the gloves for good, the King was practically penniless and had to take a travelling salesman's job to keep going.

One day he was driving from one big town to another on his tie-selling round when a speed-cop overtook him and signalled him to turn into the side of the road. 'Are you King Levinsky?' asked the policeman. Wondering what law he had broken, the former fighter acknowledged that he was. Told to telephone immediately to his home in Chicago, he drove to the nearest garage and made the call. When he hung up the receiver, he took out a handkerchief. 'Bad news?' asked the proprietor. Levinsky answered: 'Lena's gone. The Queen's dead and I ain't the King no more.'

4

He Flirted
to an Early Death

Stanley Ketchel

The only time Walter Dipley made the headlines was the day he pushed a double-barrelled shotgun through the kitchen window of a Montana ranch-house and killed Stanislaus Kiecal. That was in 1910 and it shocked the sporting world; the boxing fraternity remembered it for a long, long time, because the murdered man was the reigning middleweight champion, the most colourful character the division had ever known.

He fought under the name of Stanley Ketchel, and at that time was on top of the world. Champion at twenty, he had won, lost and re-won the title, had knocked the light-heavyweight champion cold, and sensationally put the heavyweight champion down for a count. In seven short years of fighting he had displayed hitting power that had to be seen to be believed. Only 13 of his 61 contests had gone the distance. When his leather-clad fists caressed a chin the owner went out like a light. Few got up once they had gone down from one of his pet punches.

Kiecal was born of Polish immigrant parents at Grand Rapids. His father was a farm labourer and at fifteen young Stan found himself destined to a clod-hopping life far from the bright lights of the cities where life would be a lot more exciting. His great longing was to be a cowboy, to ride the ranges, bust bronchos and herd cattle. He wanted a six-shooter on each hip, a wide Stetson, a gay-coloured neck cloth, high heels, and spurs. He wanted to ride into town with a pay-roll, spend it in the saloons and gambling halls, shoot up the place and ride out again.

So he left home and rode the rails into the West until he

reached the State of Montana. On the way he worked and fought for his food; in the mining town of Butte he chanced on a profession that was to bring him to his boyish heart's desire. The main attraction of a visiting fair was a boxing booth, at which ten dollars could be earned by staying three rounds with the star pugilist of the show.

Young Kiecal, watching eagerly with his hands thrust into his empty trouser pockets, decided to try his luck. He was both tough and strong; he knew he carried a kick in his fists that had floored many a belligerent hobo. He won the ten dollars with a single punch. After that his destiny was settled. From the travelling booths he quickly graduated into the boxing halls in the Western towns; soon his fame spread to the great fight centres of California, and finally to the mighty Cities of the East.

His Polish name proved too much of a mouthful for the average ring announcer. One day a small-time promoter altered it to Stanley Ketchel. Little did he dream that he was creating a name that would rocket across the sports pages and made sensational fight history.

By the time he was twenty they were calling him the 'Michigan Assassin'. One by one he beat down the contenders for the middleweight title, until only he and Joe Thomas disputed the championship. They fought 20 gruelling rounds to a draw that satisfied neither of them. Thomas suggested a fight to finish and two months later they waged 32 torrid rounds until Joe was counted out. Even then he was not satisfied that Ketchel was his master, so they fought for the third time, with Thomas again the loser.

The twin brothers Sullivan, Mike and Jack, challenged the new champion. Mike had first go, and on his way to the dressing-room Ketchel saw Sullivan's chief second with a large bag of oranges. 'Sam, have you bin robbing a fruit stall?' grinned Stanley. 'They're for Mike,' came the reply. 'He likes to suck the stuffin' out of half an orange between rounds. I'm cuttin' 'em up for him before we go in the ring.'

'Cut only one up,' advised the champ. 'And eat half yourself. The rest you can send back to the fruit merchant, you won't need 'em.' Mike was knocked out in eighty seconds.

Trembling with rage, brother Jack took the ring to get revenge for his brother's humiliating defeat. He was determined to go the full twenty rounds and uphold the family prestige.

Unfortunately he told the Press of his intentions and Ketchel got to hear of it. He gave Jack a systematic beating for round after round and each time Sullivan came from his corner, the Assassin greeted him with: 'What, you still hanging around, Jack? Do you think you're going to stay the distance?' Sullivan used the ring, boxed on the defensive and covered up whenever trapped against the ropes. But it was no use. Ketchel left it to the last moment and knocked him out with only a minute to go of the final round.

When he knocked Jim Smith flat on his back with a terrific right swing, Stanley vaulted over the ropes before the referee started counting and went straight to his dressing-room. He did not even look over his shoulder to see if his victim was stirring. He knew Smith was out cold.

There was also the time when he put away Hugo Kelly in three rounds. As his rival lay motionless on the ring floor, his seconds sprinkled water over him in the hopes of bringing him back to consciousness, an illegality that caused Ketchel's manager to scream with indignation. But Stanley was coolness personified. He strode over to his own corner, picked up the water bucket and swished the contents over the prostrate Kelly. 'See, he's out cold,' he said. 'He can't even swim.'

Stanley had charm, the physique of a Greek god, and when he stripped off his dressing-gown the women at the ringside gasped in admiration. He rippled his muscles at them as he stood in his corner for the starting gong; they swarmed round his dressing-room after he came back victorious. He liked that, revelled in it, and being young, full of vim and confidence, he took the fullest advantage of this lavish feminine popularity, which was not in his best interests as a fighting man.

Billy Papke, the Illinois Thunderbolt, came next. He worked out a way of beating the Assassin. It proved highly successful. When they came from their corners at the start of the fight, Stanley had a smile on his handsome face and held his hand out for the customary shake. Instead of touching gloves, Billy smote his rival hard between the eyes with a powerful right and Ketchel dropped face forwards like a log.

Somehow he managed to beat the count, but when he got to his feet it was seen that both his eyes were closing rapidly. He was put down again and again in that first three minutes, and only sheer guts enabled him to last out to the bell. After that Papke had a blind man to deal with, and he punished the game champion so severely that by the twelfth round, with Ketchel unable to see or defend himself, the referee belatedly called a halt.

The lust for revenge bit deep into the Assassin's heart, but Papke would not listen to the suggestion of a return fight. So Ketchel had to resort to subterfuge. He had the news circulated that the defeat by Papke and the loss of his title had ruined him as a fighting force; that he was now a mere shell of his former invincible self. Then he persuaded a San Francisco promoter to offer a substantial purse for a return match.

Billy fell for the decline story and Ketchel never trained harder for a fight. He could have knocked out his hated rival in the third round and any succeeding round, but he battered away without applying the closure until Papke was a helpless hulk. Then he knocked him out with a single punch in the eleventh.

No other middleweight ever dared step into the same ring with Ketchel after that. They sent for him to fight the light-heavyweight champion, Jack O'Brien, in New York. Stanley's day had arrived. He came into town wearing his cowboy outfit as happy as a lark. When he sat down at a restaurant table, he pulled a huge gun from his belt and laid it by his plate. He startled promoters by slapping this weapon on the table when they were talking business; he flourished it in the company of others. There was a big grin on his face when he fired it at someone's toes in the training camp. He slept with it under his pillow.

O'Brien was a fine boxer. He towered over Ketchel and outweighed him by a full stone. For twenty rounds he dodged the Assassin's big punches and built up a points lead, but

Stanley never gave up trying. With eight seconds to go to the final bell, he landed the one blow he had been trying for all the evening. It caught the Irishman flush on the chin and knocked him flat on his back, his head through the ropes.

They could have counted a hundred without O'Brien moving a muscle, but before the referee could reach the fatal 'out', the timekeeper rang the bell to end the fight and so save the light-heavyweight champion from an humiliating defeat.

Jack Johnson was heavyweight champion, some say he was the greatest of them all. He was a 14-st. giant and a superlative boxer. He had just licked Jim Jeffries and as a result was the most hated man in the world. When Ketchel had the audacity to challenge the coloured champion the news was electrifying. None imagined that Stanley stood a ghost of a chance, everyone hoped he would succeed. It was David and Goliath all over again – had Ketchel the winning slingshot?

Johnson grinned his way through the first eleven rounds, making the smaller man miss, almost playing with him. But Ketchel wiped the smile off his dusky face in the twelfth with a mighty right that sent the heavyweight champion toppling to the canvas. As Johnson went down all the fans stood up. Ketchel leaned against the ropes, there was murder in his steely-blue eyes. Jack scrambled to his feet, shook his head to clear away the cobwebs – and Ketchel charged in for the 'kill'.

He ran full tilt into a right uppercut that almost tore his head from his shoulders. It picked Stanley up as if he was a feather and stretched him out on the ring floor like a huge starfish. He had to be carried to his corner, and when Johnson got to his dressing-room they found three of Ketchel's teeth imbedded in his glove.

There was every excuse for defeat; in fact, Ketchel's prestige mounted even higher. The fans clamoured for a second bout between them and Stanley was only too willing. Colonel R.P. Pickerson, one of Ketchel's keenest supporters, owned a ranch at Conway in Missouri and invited the boxer to go there for a holiday before starting serious training for the return bout with Johnson. Here he would be in his element and could play the cowboy to his heart's content. Everything was laid on for him.

A bright, airy bedroom, the run of the ranch, riding, swimming, fishing, hunting. A wonderful opportunity to tone up to physical perfection.

Then he met Goldie Smith. She was blonde and beautiful, something Ketchel had not expected to encounter in the Pickerson place. She was cook-housekeeper and in charge of the boxer's meals. One look at Stanley's handsome countenance and there wasn't enough she could do for him. Ketchel grinned; it was too easy, there wouldn't be any harm in playing around a bit. They were thrown together a lot during the day when the ranch hands were out on the range. But Ketchel flirted with her openly at any time it suited him, ignoring the black looks he got from Walter Dipley, the foreman.

To Stanley it was a passing joke, but Goldie took it very seriously. Dipley had been her boy friend before the arrival of Ketchel, now she brushed off the foreman's attentions. The fighter was famous. He was champion of the world with the greatest knockout record ever known. She was flattered whenever he took notice of her and Dipley knew he didn't stand a chance.

The girl meant nothing to Ketchel, but when he realised how intolerably jealous Dipley had become, Stanley went out of his way to pull the foreman's leg. He infuriated Dipley and made him suspicious whenever Goldie and he were left alone in the ranchhouse. To Stanley it was such a joke that he failed to see the murderous look of hate that began to show in Dipley's eyes.

One morning Ketchel came down to breakfast after the ranch hands and cowboys had gone off on the day's routine. It was a meal Goldie had taken great pains to prepare and decidedly more inviting than the one she had put before the foreman a couple of hours earlier. Ketchel was almost ready to leave the Pickerson ranch. He had wired Willus Britt, his manager, saying he was tremendously fit, and inviting him to come out and see for himself. Britt was expected that day and Stanley was excited at the prospect of fighting again, this time for the biggest purse of his colourful career.

He was in high spirits. He slipped his arm round Goldie's

waist, pulled her down to him and gave her a spanking kiss. Neither of them heard Walter Dipley approach the open window behind them. Goldie giggled and darted off, Ketchel kissed his big right fist, a characteristic gesture, then picked up his knife and got to work on his breakfast.

Through the window was thrust a double-barrelled shotgun. Dipley pressed the triggers of both barrels and Ketchel took the full charge in his back. The stricken fighter tried to stand up, grabbed at the table and pitched in a heap on the floor. Dipley ran into the room, seized Ketchel's valuable tiepin and diamond ring, snatched his wallet containing 500 dollars and darted out. Jumping on a waiting horse, he was away, leaving Goldie screaming for help.

Miraculously they found the fighter still alive and he was rushed to hospital. The news was flashed round the world and in New York a sports editor remarked to his boxing writer: 'Looks as though Ketchel will die; he's in hospital full of gunshot wounds.' 'If they start to count ten over him, he'll get up,' said the fight scribe.

But he didn't. A few hours later the great Michigan Assassin was dead, and Ketchel's family, father and brothers, offered 5,000 dollars for Dipley's dead body; they weren't interested in having him caught alive. It wasn't long before the hunted man was brought to the sheriff at the point of a farmer's shotgun. The Ketchels paid the reward, but were disappointed when a jury sentenced Dipley to life imprisonment in the Missouri State penitentiary.

He stayed there 23 years, by which time the shock of Stanley's sudden death had been softened. But Ketchel had not been forgotten and never will be by those who follow the Fight Game. He died when at the very zenith of his career, just three months past his 23rd birthday, all because the killer of the ring fancied himself as a lady killer.

5

Mother-Love
Kept Him from the Top

Young Stribling

Had it not been for his mother's loving care, Young Stribling, the Georgia heavyweight, might easily have been champion of the world. He had the physique and the ability; he had the courage and he had the opportunities. Not that she objected to him being a fighter. Once she realised that he loved the ring and revelled in boxing, she became his greatest booster. Yet she was always scared that something dreadful might happen to him.

When he was fighting someone of little account, she would send him out with the encouraging chant: 'Get that bum, Will, quick as you like', and he'd put his opponent away with artistic ease. But, if the opposition was dangerous and the occasion of vital importance to his career, she'd change her tune and yell: 'Be careful now, Will, don't get hurt.' And once again he would take heed – and be so careful that he failed to win.

His parents were travelling acrobats of quality, and when he was born on Boxing Day 1904, they called him William Lawrence, the first name after his father and the second after the great John Lawrence Sullivan, first of the world's heavyweight champions. Pa Stribling was an ardent boxing fan and he took his son to see famous fights almost as soon as he could toddle. When a second boy was born he was christened Herbert, but always called 'Babe'. He was sparring with Young Bill before he could talk.

Right from childhood, the brothers were taught tumbling and acrobatic tricks; eventually they joined their parents in the act. As midget boxers, the two Stribling boys were an added attraction. Pa watched Young Bill develop into a proficient

boxer with keen interest, but Ma thought fighting was dangerous. She reminded her husband that in their business they took
the falls without getting badly hurt because it was part of their
training, but in the Fight Game their son could get damaged
both mentally and physically. Pa argued that the boy wanted to
be a fighter and thought of nothing else. He suggested that they
should give him a run and promised he would not be allowed
to come to any harm.

So at 16 Young Stribling was launched as a professional, and
was soon earning a reputation in the Central and Southern
States. Pa was manager and trainer, Ma watched over his
physical welfare and diet, Babe acted as chief sparring-partner.
Bill made such progress that the acrobatic act was dissolved
and his fighting career became a family concern.

On fight nights, Ma worked in the dressing-room with the
others and she walked down the aisle behind Willie, Pa and
Babe, but she never climbed into the ring. She sat directly
behind her son's corner, and everybody in the arena knew she
was there. She was neither shy or soft-voiced. Every precaution
was taken to see that no bodily harm befell the breadwinner.
His opponents were chosen with the greatest care; in fact,
many of them were part and parcel of the 'circus', being sent
on in advance to 'challenge' the 'Boy Wonder' on his arrival in
the next town.

This went on for several years and then the sports-minded
among the Georgians suddenly realised they had a real
personality in their midst. They decided to lose no time in
exploiting it and Mike McTigue was invited to come to
Columbus and defend his world's light-heavyweight title. The
champion accepted with the proviso that he brought his own
referee and was paid 17,500 dollars. The Georgians thought
this a cheap way of gaining a world crown for their idol and
McTigue duly arrived. He was a cagey old fighter, who exerted
himself as little as possible to win his contests. Young
Bill – not yet nineteen – was urged by his mother to take no
risks. The result was that it was about the poorest championship contest ever seen.

At the finish the referee called it a 'draw', a fair verdict. It meant that Mike had kept his crown and this was more than the disappointed ringsiders could stand. Among them were members of the dreaded Ku Klux Klan, who climbed into the ring waving revolvers and insisting that Stribling be announced as the winner, whereupon the referee was so scared that he altered his decision, and Young Bill was fêted as the new champion. But his triumph was short-lived. As soon as he got back to New York the referee gave his 'official' verdict as a 'draw'; that is how it appears in the record books.

Three years later Stribling got another crack at the title, this time against Paul Berlanbach, who had succeeded McTigue. The champion had the reputation of being a big puncher, and again Mrs Stribling urged her son to take every care. He carried it to extremes and at the end of fifteen rounds Berlanbach had scarcely laid a glove on him, simply because Stribling had kept at a safe distance. But Ma was satisfied that he had picked up a good-sized purse and come out without a scratch.

So, too, was Bill's young bride, pretty Clara Virginia, daughter of a wealthy cotton broker, who was just as anxious that her husband's handsome features should not be spoiled by fighting. She formed the Stribling Realty Company, with herself as General Manager and Pa, Ma and Babe as directors. By this time Young Bill had taken part in 120 contests and was still only 21. Most of the critics considered that to pack so much action into five years had burned the fighting spirit out of Stribling, and that that was why he boxed so poorly in important contests; the family had other ideas. They travelled through the majority of the States in an almost continuous tour. In 1927 he had 20 contests, the following year no less than 38. But the bulk of these bouts were against fighters of small account, who lasted only a round or two. Meanwhile, the Stribling reputation was being rebuilt, and soon he was ready for the big stuff again.

They matched him with Jack Sharkey at Miami, the millionaire winter resort, the winner being promised a match with Gene Tunney for the heavyweight title. Again there were frenzied urgings from his mother to be careful. Sharkey was a notoriously rough fighter, capable of any trick that might cause permanent damage to a man.

Young Bill nodded, but this was a wonderful chance and he meant to make the most of it. He boxed with great caution until near the end of the first round, then opened out and landed four vicious rights to the chin that dropped his rival in a heap.

It looked all over, but the tough Sharkey was saved by the bell and when he got back to his corner Stribling received a severe scolding for being so reckless. The fans, who had watched in amazement as Stribling lashed out, soon realised that it was just a flash in the pan. For the rest of the contest Young Bill relied on sheer defensive tactics and was adjudged the loser. Next day one of the boxing writers renamed him 'Willie the Clutch'.

When the decision was given to Sharkey, Ma Stribling really blew her top. She leaned far over the ring apron and screamed at the referee, denouncing him as a crook and villain. Front-row spectator Al Capone was most impressed with her vitriolic outburst. The famous Chicago gangster grinned and told his neighbours: 'She's got more guts than my whole mob.'

Promoter Jeff Dickson brought him to London where he fought a sensational contest with Primo Carnera at the Albert Hall. The whole family came too, with the addition of William Stribling the Third, his three-year old son, who sat on his mother's lap next to grandma and Uncle Babe, while grandpop was up in the corner with daddy. There was no need for anyone to tell him to be careful this time. At 6ft 5¾in. Carnera towered above him, while he was outweighed by about eighty pounds. Yet he felt confident that he could outbox the giant Italian who was little more than a novice.

That is how it was until the third round when, seeing Carnera's enormous chin completely unguarded, Stribling took a pot shot at it with a swift right-hander and sent the big man crashing to the canvas. Dazed as he was, Primo sprang up and caught the American by surprise with a powerful right swing that knocked him clean off his feet. Now there was real panic in the Stribling corner. Young Bill was down and the whole family screamed at him to get up. He beat the count and kept on his feet until the bell sounded. Then in the next round, he swung wildly at the big man, landed a decidedly low blow, and was promptly disqualified.

When Stribling returned to England in 1930 and knocked out Phil Scott, the British champion, in two rounds, he earned himself a fight with Max Schmeling for the world's title. The German had created a record by being the first man to win the championship whilst on the canvas, Sharkey having been ruled out in round four for an alleged foul. Schmeling had not fought since and had gone unchallenged for over a year. He and Stribling were matched to fight on 3 July 1931 at Cleveland, Ohio.

Strangely enough, although his mother was deeply concerned about him coming to harm in the ring, she paid no attention to his daring in other directions. He drove high-powered cars when travelling from one fight venue to another, and for longer distances used a small plane.

One day, when Schmeling was doing some training in public, Stribling flew over the camp at a very low altitude, banking and stunting, coming down to tree-top level again and again. If he thought this would scare the German champion, he was very much mistaken. But it frightened the life out of the promoters, who brought an injunction restraining Young Bill from taking such risks.

'This is my big chance,' he told his mother as he climbed into the ring. 'So let me fight this one my own way.' 'Okay, Will,' she replied. But the old warning to be careful he had heard so many times when leaving his corner had become so ingrained in his mind and muscles, he just could not let himself go.

Although he put up the fight of his life, Stribling was hopelessly beaten and the whole family watched him take a terrible hiding in silence. In the 14th round Schmeling battered him into the canvas, and although Stribling struggled up, the referee would not let a game man take further punishment.

Stribling's purse had been over 33,000 dollars. He owned considerable property in Georgia, and was running a successful fruit farm. There was no need for him to fight again. But Stribling was not ready to retire yet. He was only 26 and knew no other profession, so the boxing circus continued until his wife dropped out because another child was about due. Stribling left her at their home in Macon while he went to Houston in Texas to outpoint Maxie Rosenbloom.

A few days later news reached him that he was a father, so he borrowed a motor cycle and set off to rejoin his family. The powerful machine ate up the miles as the fighter got the last ounce of speed out of it. He was almost home when he ran straight into a fast car coming towards him. He was barely alive when they picked him up, his right foot being severed above the ankle, his ribs crushed, his pelvis and spine damaged.

Ma Stribling was at the hospital bedside, imploring the doctors to save her boy. All the care and caution she had urged on him from boyhood had not saved him from that fatal moment on the road. 'Sorry, Ma,' he said with a faint grin. 'I shoulda been more careful.' Then he turned his face away, and died.

6

Illicit Love
Cost Him his Life

George Stevenson

If you are a big, tough fighter and want to become Champion of England, it isn't always an asset to be good-looking as well. It may be nice to be thought handsome and the centre of feminine admiration, but it can also bring you to ruin. That is what George Stevenson, the burly Yorkshire coachman found. He had what it takes to reach the top in the fistic profession and had his big chance. But he stepped out of his class and paid the full penalty. In fact, it cost him his life.

A strong, well-muscled youth, Stevenson had found employment at the home of Richard Sykes, a wealthy merchant who maintained a magnificent mansion at Sledmere. It was George's job to keep the stables clean, wash and polish the carriages, and exercise the horses. His work kept him busy for most of the day, yet he found time to indulge in sports, and before long gained a reputation for being adept at quarter-staffs, broadswords and fisticuffs, the rough and ready recreations of the working classes in England two hundred years ago.

By the time he was eighteen, Stevenson was generally regarded as Champion of Yorkshire at these athletic pursuits; he might never have left Sledmere but for an attack of gout. Not that George suffered: the painful affliction descended on the under-coachman, but it changed the whole course of the stable-lad's life.

Much to the relief of his young and beautiful second wife, Mr Sykes had gone to London on business, being driven by his head coachman with two footmen in attendance. In his absence came an invitation to attend a county ball thrown by some friends living about ten miles away. Bored to tears by being cooped up with an old man, the lady of the house decided to go by herself.

She sent for the under-coachman and ordered him to prepare for the journey. Timidly he explained that his foot was so swollen with gout that he could not possibly drive. 'There must surely be someone else?' demanded Mrs Sykes, and when it was explained that only the stable-lad was available, she gave instructions that he should dress himself suitably and make the journey.

She gave a start when she saw the handsome, well-built youth up on the box when she entered the coach. She was also pleasantly surprised at the way he handled the two spirited horses and the speed at which the trip was made. Her lone arrival caused some comment, but her beauty, low-cut gown and glittering diamonds made her the star of the ball. When, at midnight, the coach was ready to take her home, she kept it waiting for as long as she dared and had many gallant volunteers to accompany her on the journey, the dangers of travelling in the early hours of the morning being stressed as an excuse.

Mrs Sykes was quite content to return the way she had come, however. She glanced up at young Stevenson, assured her friends she was in good hands and they set off in the moonlight. Halfway back, as they clattered along the frosty road, George saw a horseman emerge from a cluster of trees ahead of him, then a second and a third. Obviously they were there to intercept anyone coming from the county ball. There would be valuable jewellery to be had for the taking. Slipping masks over their faces, they formed a barrier across the road.

It was a time for quick thinking and rapid action. Stevenson whipped the horses into a gallop, wrapped the reins round his left hand, and snatching a long pistol from the coach holster, drove straight at the highwaymen. They slid from their mounts and scattered, but George shot one of them down, and while his fair passenger screamed with fear, he pulled the horses to a standstill and leapt from the box to chase after the two remaining bandits.

One attempted to fire, but the coachman smashed his face in

with the pistol butt, then chased after the other man, grabbed him by the shoulder, spun him round and knocked him senseless with a powerful blow to the jaw. Back to the coach he found his mistress had been thoroughly scared and although it took time to calm her down, they continued the journey without further unpleasant incident.

When her husband returned from London, his wife lost no time in telling him of the young stable-lad's heroism, and how he had saved both her life and her jewellery. Promptly George was promoted to under-coachman, and it was not long before he was taking his young mistress for drives around the countryside. The excursions became more frequent and of longer duration. In the absence of his employer on business trips, Stevenson spent more time in the mansion that he did in the stables. Tongues began to wag and people wondered how it was that old Mr Sykes seemed unaware of what was going on in his household.

Perhaps he did know, because on his return from London one day he called George into his study and questioned him about himself, saying that he understood that Stevenson had quite a reputation in the county as a fighting man. Indeed, he was regarded as the best in Yorkshire. Modestly the young coachman replied that so far he had not come across anyone yet who could beat him in a bare-fist bout, whereupon his employer asked if he would like to broaden his activities by going to London and challenging for the Championship.

He said there was a big opportunity for a young man of promise, that he knew the Prince of Wales (son of George the Second) was a generous patron of the Noble Art and was looking for a man who could defeat Jack Broughton, the recognised champion whom his brother, the Duke of Cumberland, was sponsoring. Stevenson was perfectly content to stay in Sledmere, but the thought of going to glamorous London under the patronage of the King's eldest son was too great a temptation.

The next day Mr Sykes wished him goodbye and good luck in his fistic adventures, while Mrs Sykes had to fight hard to keep back her tears. She pleaded with the young coachman to return to Yorkshire as soon as possible. 'He will come back when he has become Champion of England,' prophesied her husband meaningly.

As soon as he reached the great city, George found lodgings in Clerkenwell, spruced himself up, and called at the magnificent house in Leicester Square which the Prince of Wales had set up in opposition to his father's royal court at Windsor. It was a wild and carefree establishment, filled with Prince Frederick's fast-living, loose-moralled friends, who drank and gambled from darkness until dawn. The uncouth Yorkshire lad was thrown into this bizarre company, and he took to the life like a duck to water.

He gave an exhibition of his prowess in the drawing-room, his compact, muscular physique commanding great admiration; it was obvious that he knew how to take care of himself in the ring. The Prince was delighted, supplied George with plenty of money and lost no time in letting his brother know that he had found the man who had the beating of Broughton. The Champion had come from Cirencester in Gloucestershire and found work as a waterman on the River Thames. Among his rough workmates he found plenty of opportunity to develop into a proficient pugilist, eventually being taken up by James Fig, the recognised Champion of England, who had a boxing booth in Tottenham Court Road (at the Oxford Street end) where he taught the Noble Art of Self-Defence, and staged tournaments which received full support from the royal princes and their aristocratic friends.

Under Fig's tuition, Broughton became so skilled in the use of his fists that he proved far too good for any opponent that could be found for him. After he had beaten Tom Pipes and Bill Gretting, he was acclaimed as the successor to Fig as Champion of England, and for a time was reduced to giving exhibitions while waiting for his first challenger to put in an appearance. Then one morning he was greatly surprised to receive the following communication:

'Mr Broughton – You think yourself a great fighter. Perhaps you are, but there are people living in Clerkenwell who say your fighting days are over and you are good for nothing but to show off. I will meet you a month from today. If you don't come up, you are a coward. If you don't dust me, you are a humbug. If I beat you, you are a dead man.'

Quite mystified, Broughton took the challenging missive to his patron, but the Duke of Cumberland knew what it was all about. He explained that his brother had produced a Yorkshireman whom he thought would be more than a match for the Champion, even though he had never fought a man of Broughton's class. The challenge would be accepted and, following a meeting between all those concerned, it was arranged for the fight to take place in Fig's amphitheatre in February 1741. The forthcoming contest became the talk of the town, and speculation as to its outcome spread all over the country, especially in that part of Yorkshire from which Stevenson had come.

Most of The Fancy regarded the match as a touch of royal madness. None of them had ever heard of Stevenson, and to pit a novice against the accomplished Broughton was akin to sending a lamb to be slaughtered. Even George thought his Prince had aimed a bit too high as a starter. He suggested that it might be best if he first had a try-out contest with a lesser light of the ring, but His Royal Highness would not hear of it. 'Mr Sykes has given me such a glowing account of your fistic ability that I had no hesitation in issuing your challenge direct to Broughton himself,' replied Prince Frederick, adding: 'Mr Sykes is coming specially to see the bout, so you had better do your damnedest to win.'

Stevenson then realised that this was his late employer's malicious way of gaining revenge for his coachman's betrayal. But George was no coward. Furthermore he knew only too well that to withdraw from the championship fight would finish him socially throughout England. He resolved that if he had to go down, he would go down fighting.

The arena was packed to capacity when the Prince of Wales and the Duke of Cumberland came in with a retinue of lords and ladies to fill the gallery. The lords were members of the royal court, but the ladies were not. They were dressed in the height of fashion and made-up to perfection, but their remarks to the fighting men were not in keeping.

Both fighters were fine physical specimens, the Yorkshireman slightly shorter, but stockier. He was an inch or so shorter and seven or eight pounds lighter, but pleased the onlookers by attacking strongly. It was soon made clear, however, that he had nothing like the science of the Champion, who blocked his well-intended punches, stepped back and countered with tremendous blows to the body and head.

In Prize Fighting the rounds were not measured by any set length of time. They ended when one or other of the contestants was sent to the floor, either from a blow or being thrown, as wrestling was included. The fights were to a finish, they were supreme tests of endurance, all the while a man was conscious he was expected to continue the battle. Soon Stevenson was bleeding badly from the nose and mouth, but he fought on with great courage. In desperation at not being able to catch the champion with an effective blow, George tried hard to seize hold of Broughton and toss him to the boards, but Jack was also his superior at wrestling, and it was the challenger who went down heavily with the champion on top.

First success had gone to Broughton and the Duke was loud in the expression of his pleasure. He had wagered a large sum on Broughton and was confident that he would win his brother's money. But it was Frederick's turn to cheer lustily in the second round when Stevenson landed a smashing right-hand punch on the champion's nose that brought the blood flowing in streams. With characteristic coolness Jack warded off his rival's attempts to repeat the blow or land another of any account, but he had to give some ground before the game Yorkshireman's strong attack, which was receiving every encouragement from the excited onlookers eager to witness a sensational upset of form.

Suddenly Broughton darted in and grasped his opponent round the waist. Stevenson resisted strongly, but had not the skill to cope with this style of fighting and the champion was on the point of throwing the Yorkshireman when he was tripped and they both fell heavily. The fall had shaken them up, but there was only thirty seconds permitted before it would be time for toeing the line again. Stevenson was looking the worse for wear when he came up for the third round. He was staggering and Broughton, quick to notice his distress, rushed him into a corner. Holding him against the ring post in a vice-like grip, he squeezed him in his mighty arms until poor George's eyes almost popped out of his head. Then suddenly releasing his victim, Jack stepped back and delivered a terrible right-handed blow under the coachman's heart. The gallant York-shireman gave a great gasp and fell in a crumpled heap on the stage.

He did not move and Broughton knelt at his side and put his hand to his chest. 'Good God, what have I done?' he shouted. 'I've killed him! So help me, God, I'll never fight again.' That was the considered opinion of everyone present. While they carted the limp form of Stevenson out of the ring, the Prince of Wales silently handed over his purse to the Duke of Cumberland and the arena emptied, with little thought given to the stricken man beyond the fact that he had been well and truly beaten by the indomitable Broughton.

George was removed to the nearby Adam and Eve tavern where he was put to bed. It was several hours before he regained consciousness; he was then examined by a doctor, who found that two of his ribs had been broken, and that he was suffering from internal haemorrhage for which nothing could be done; he was expected to die within a few days. In fact he lived on for nearly a month, during which time he asked that Broughton should pay him a visit. The distressed champion came to his side and the pair shook hands. Jack continued to come and chat with his dying opponent until the end.

The Fancy gave Stevenson a magnificent funeral, and among the many floral tributes was a beautiful wreath that had been sent by special post-chaise from Sledmere. As for Broughton, he did fight again, but not before he had drawn up the first set of Rules for the Prize Ring, conditions that prevented anyone from beating an opponent to death in the manner in which he himself had used to defeat poor George Stevenson. These rules remained, modified from time to time, for more than a hundred years, at which time the Marquess of Queensberry gave his name to those that stipulated the use of gloves and so saw the finish of the Prize Ring.

7

White Women were his Ruin

Jack Johnson

Many boxing experts maintain that Jack Johnson was the greatest of all the heavyweight champions of the world. A superb ring craftsman throughout every inch of his glistening ebony frame, he was also a master of defence and a destructive puncher. Yet, he was the most hated man ever to pull on a pair of gloves, mainly because of his endless pursuits of white women – an unpardonable offence in his day. There were plenty of coloured girls in Jack's life while he was fighting his way to the top, but once he had beaten Tommy Burns to become the first black man to hold the world's title, he scorned his own race, both male and female.

Jack had to chase Burns round the world before he could force him into a championship defence at Sydney, Australia. Tommy was strong, an excellent boxer, a heavy hitter. Yet the coloured man toyed with him before the police climbed into the ring during the 14th round and stopped a one-sided contest. Had Johnson kept his head and behaved as a world's champion should, his reign as titleholder would have been a lot less harassed and far more lucrative. But he flaunted himself as a superman with such arrogant showmanship that the boxing fraternity went frantic in an effort to find a white man who could beat him.

That was the start of the 'White Hope' era that proved a grim joke for nearly seven years. It brought the hitherto unbeaten Jim Jeffries out of retirement, to suffer a humiliating defeat that caused race riots throughout America; Johnson's unpopularity reached an unparalleled peak. His enemies set out to destroy him. If they couldn't get him beaten inside the ring, they would do so outside the ropes or in his private life. And Jack played right into their hands with a succession of dubious affairs with the womenfolk of his acquaintance.

His first marriage was to Mary Austin, a Galveston coloured girl, who left him after three years. He then had tempestuous affairs with Etta Reynolds and Clara Kerr, two others of his own race, that brought him adverse publicity. During this time he was rapidly becoming recognised as a dangerous threat to the heavyweight title, and when Tommy Burns went to London to defend his crown against Gunner James Moir, Johnson chased after him.

The money for the trip was supplied by a New York Irishman, whose daughter, Hattie McLay, was infatuated with the big coloured boxer. There was some raising of eyebrows when Jack appeared in London with her hanging on his arm and a lot of disapproval when she accompanied him to Australia and sat at the ringside to watch him win the championship from Burns. But Hattie and Jack broke up when he returned to America and another white girl, Belle Screiber, teamed up with him and they travelled together from State to State as he fulfilled his many boxing engagements. When he went to San Francisco to defend the title against Stanley Ketchel, they found Miss McLay waiting for them, and while Jack was knocking out the middleweight champion in twelve rounds, the two women were battling it out in his hotel.

Johnson fled to New York and at a theatre there met Etta Duryea, a married white woman. She was fascinated by him, and it appealed to Johnson's vanity to start a romantic courtship. Within a few days she ran away from her husband and stayed with Jack in Pittsburgh until her divorce was finalised. Then he made her his second bride and they spent the honeymoon on a liner bound for London.

Once more he revelled in the unpopular publicity and encountered his first real setback since becoming champion. A promoting syndicate was prepared to pay him a large sum to defend his title against Bombardier Billy Wells, the British titleholder, but the Home Office banned the contest. The official reason was the fear of racial disturbances in the British

Empire, but behind it was the determination of the National Sporting Club, which had been badly treated by Johnson on his previous visit, to prevent him from boxing in England. So Jack had to be content with music-hall engagements, and his London hotel breathed with relief when he and his white wife departed for America, even though their bill was unsettled.

Promoter Tex Rickard paid Jeffries a fortune to come out of a five-year retirement in an effort to recapture the heavyweight title for the white race, and he earned every penny of it. Johnson jeered at his efforts to land a big punch and systematically cut him to pieces, punishing the older man so severely that the referee had to intervene in the 15th round to prevent Big Jim from being counted out.

Johnson was hooted from the ring, although he had won fairly and squarely. In the next two years he fought only once, a victory over Jim Flynn at Las Vegas that barely got into the papers. Two months later, however, his name was blazoned across every front page. His wife, Etta, committed suicide, shooting herself in their Chicago home and leaving a note that put Jack in a very bad light.

Did he take heed? Almost immediately his name was coupled with a 19-year-old white Minnesota girl, Lucille Cameron, who ran off with him posing as his secretary; in less than three months after the death of his second wife, Johnson had married his third. Lucille's mother brought a charge of abduction against the coloured champion, now aged 34, but his enemies went one better. They raked up his affair with Belle Screiber and to Johnson's alarm he found himself charged under the Mann Act, a law that forbid the transportation of a woman from one State to another for immoral purposes.

He was sentenced to a year and a day's imprisonment, plus a fine of 5,000 dollars, but was allowed to appeal and released on bail in the sum of 30,000 dollars. Jack knew that once he was in prison his title would be forfeited and he would never enter a ring again. There was only one thing to be done. His must flee the country. He and his girl-wife crossed into Canada and left Montreal on the liner *Corinthia* and sailed for Europe.

Johnson was an outlaw from his own country for almost two

years and was tricked into returning by being promised that his sentence would be quashed if he agreed to defend his title against Jess Willard, a giant cowboy from Kansas. The coloured champion was 37 now, ring-rusty and sadly out of condition after a life of gay living in Paris. He hated being an exile, as did his wife; also he wanted to see his aged mother.

He signed the contract knowing full well that it was for a fight he was certain of losing. It was scheduled for 45 rounds and Jack knew he would never last that long. So he demanded a fee of 50,000 dollars and a share of the motion-picture proceeds. The fight was staged on the Havana race track in Cuba. Part of the promised purse was paid to Johnson before he entered the ring, the remainder was to be handed to his wife as soon as it had been taken at the box-office.

Lucille sat waiting in the ringside seat, ready to give her husband the sign that he could end the contest as soon as he liked. Jack thought this might be about the 10th round, at which stage he still stood a chance of scoring a knockout. But the promoters were too clever for that.

They could see that despite his long absence from the ring, Johnson was outboxing his big challenger in the early rounds, gliding round him, jabbing to the face, hammering him to the body at close range. Several times he planted a hard right on the cowboy's big chin, but Jack was six inches shorter and having to hit upwards took a lot of the power out of his punches. The longer he was kept in the ring the better, so they held up the payment of the final instalment of his money.

He staggered Willard more than once, and by the 10th round, Big Jess was well behind on points and seemed tired. Johnson also was feeling weary. He kept glancing at Lucille, hoping to see her give him the okay sign, but her hands remained in her lap and she had to shake her head. Jack fought on, still scoring the bulk of the points, but with gloom in his heart. The promoters were holding back the money, keeping it until he was almost exhausted. He dare not end the fight himself, although it was probably within his power to do so at this stage. He had to plod on in the hopes that when at last Lucille had the money he would not be too far gone to win.

At the 23rd round, and only half-way through the contest, Johnson could barely raise his arms. His punches had become woolly, and it began to dawn on Willard that Jack could not hurt him. Jess started to do some attacking himself and was amazed when a long left swing to the head sent the champion staggering. Willard went after him and now Jack was fighting desperately to keep on his feet. Through the next two rounds Willard kept up the pressure and the fans were now roaring at the cowboy to finish off the black man. Johnson half saw a movement at the ringside. Lucille was standing up. She held a packet in her hand and waved it, then made her way out of the arena.

Now Jack called on his last reserves of strength, and went after Willard, but the giant challenger was fighting with full confidence now. Midway through the 26th round, he swung a tremendous uppercut from his knees that caught the oncoming champion full on the point of the chin. Down went Johnson. He rolled over on to his back, his gloves went up to protect his glazed eyes from the blazing sun, and they counted him out. He had lost his title, but if Jack thought his troubles were over, he was sadly mistaken. No sooner had he stepped on American soil, then he was arrested and committed to prison to serve the sentence passed on him seven years earlier.

The society he had flouted through his blatant association with white women had gained full revenge. He was never again permitted to fight in the United States and, after serving his time in Leavenworth Jail, he came out to suffer the hardest knock of all. He was no longer champion, no longer able to earn a living as a professional boxer. He was an ex-criminal and Lucille, no longer attracted to him, took quick steps to secure a divorce. And for the last twelve years of his life, until he was killed in a car accident in 1946, the great Jack Johnson lived an almost hand-to-mouth existence.

8

Mother was the World's Strongest Woman

Ted Sandwina

If you want to be a heavyweight boxing champion and your mother happens to be the Strongest Woman in the World, your prospects should be regarded as considerable. Not so, however, in the case of Teddy Sandwina, the young German-American who made an impressive impact in London rings towards the end of the 1920s.

Kati Brumbach was born in a caravan in Alsace-Lorraine. Her German parents performed in a travelling circus and they soon brought her into the act. At the age of two she could do handstands, and when she was sixteen she had developed into such a remarkable physical specimen that her father offered a hundred marks to any man who could pin her shoulders in a wrestling match.

There were plenty of takers, but no winners, and one day in Saxony a young acrobat named Max Heymann took up the challenge. He fared no better than the rest; within seconds he had been picked up and slammed on the canvas. He lay so still that Kati imagined she had done him an injury and bent down to enquire if he was all right. To her surprise he looked up, grinned, and said: 'I love you. Will you marry me?' It was the strong girl's first proposal. She gasped, blushed and whispered: 'Pretend you can't get up.' Then she lifted him off the floor, held him at arm's length and carried him out of the arena.

They eloped to Norway and were married, then Kati and her husband created their own act and toured the world. At full maturity she stood 6ft 0¾in. and weighed 210 pounds, her vital statistics being 43-29-43. Each morning she kept in training by holding her 5ft 5in., 154-pound husband aloft, lowering and pressing him up again six times with either hand. As part of the publicity she claimed to have defeated the renowned Eugen Sandow in feats of strength and afterwards called herself Sandwina, the World's Strongest Woman. With Max she went to America, and in 1909 at Sioux City, Iowa, she did her two performances one day, went back to her lodgings and gave birth to a son.

They named him Theodore and claimed he was a godson to that tempestuous President of the United States, Theodore Roosevelt. At two he also could perform handstands, and in due course developed into a strong and powerful youth with a penchant for boxing. Kati was a bit perturbed about this decisive departure from legitimate show business. Teddy was fair, curly-haired and very handsome, and it pained her to think that his face might suffer disfigurement at the hands of others. She loved him with deep intensity, but would not stand in his way. He grew to be 6ft 1in. in height and weigh almost 200 pounds. Her diminutive husband thought he was big enough to look after himself and she had to agree.

In Germany, where they were on tour, they encountered a West Indian boxer with the colourful name of Rocky Knight. He was a well-known performer in British rings, and at that time was acting as sparring partner to German fighters and taking what bouts came his way. He undertook to teach young Sandwina all he knew. It wasn't a lot, but was enough for Ted to make a start among the up-and-coming locals with a consistent run of success.

Then Kati received an offer to appear in the annual circus at Olympia and the whole family came to London. That was in December 1926, when boxing was having a terrific boom in this country, and it gave Ted his big opportunity. At Premierland in London's East End, they ran three shows a week; consequently new talent was always welcome. Even so, the proprietors, Messrs Victor Berliner and Manny Littlestone, could hardly believe their eyes when Kati walked in and started to talk about engagements.

At first they had the horrifying idea that she was out with a personal challenge to Phil Scott, the British heavyweight champion. She was certainly big enough, but through her broken English they discovered that she was talking about her son, and when she brought him in they could hardly believe their eyes. Here indeed was a gift from the gods; within minutes they had fixed terms (somewhat low it may be added) for Teddy to box there the following Sunday afternoon, having assured his mother that he would come to no harm. 'If he does,' purred Mr Berliner, 'you will know whether or not he has any future as a fighter.' And Mr Littlestone added that to give him every encouragement they would be prepared to engage him for six bouts on the understanding that his exclusive services belonged to them.

Fred Young, of Marylebone, was to be the first burnt offering, and with an array of clowns, acrobats and bare-back riders, Ma wedged herself into a ringside seat and waited for her beloved son to do his stuff. Ted did his best, tried a right that should have knocked his opponent into the Commercial Road, missed, and was promptly punched on the nose with a straight left.

Kati gasped and roared at Young like a wounded elephant. It put the Marylebone man right out of his stride and for the next ten rounds he did nothing but make Sandwina miss. Had he stuck to his left leads he must have won by a mile, but in the last minute of the fight, Ma bellowed again and turning to look, Fred took a right smash on the chin and went down for the full count.

So Teddy got away to a good start and in the course of the next six weeks filled Premierland to capacity by stopping Harry Reeve, Joe Mullings, Eddie Riches, Jack Stanley and Tom Norris in a mere matter of nineteen incompleted rounds. Messrs B. & L. then lent him out to the Albert Hall where he drew with Con O'Kelly over ten rounds, and outpointed him over fifteen; by now the Press boys were prophesying that ex-President Roosevelt's godson was moving fast towards a fight for the world's title.

A misguided and over-zealous admirer thought it would be a good idea if Sandwina took on George Cook, the veteran Australian who had been fighting for so many years he did his boxing by sheer memory. Cook couldn't punch and he lacked real fistic skill, but he could fiddle his way to victory over men younger and more talented than himself. If the Sandwina camp imagined he would provide another victim for Teddy they were hopelessly mistaken.

Cook plunged straight into battle, taking the young German completely out of his stride. Sandwina had to absorb a number of left hooks and swings to the side of the head and almost immediately sustained a cut close to his right eye. The veteran played on the wound when he was not assailing the body and Teddy was bustled around without being able to do much in return. Pursuing the same tactics in the second round, the Australian had the better of things until in the final minutes Sandwina banged in some heavy lefts to the older man's body and rocked him back on his heels with a perfect straight left. It seemed as though Sandwina had settled down by the third round, for he caught his rival with some telling shots. Then another swinging left opened his eye injury, and with blood streaming down his face Teddy was in no state to continue; the referee wisely called a halt. When Sandwina's wound had healed they met again, this time over fifteen rounds at the famous Ring at Blackfriars; once again Old George knew too much for his vigorous young opponent, winning a points decision with ridiculous ease.

Further successes for Sandwina followed, however. Marcel Nilles of France was stopped in three rounds, then came quick defeats for Henri Rogers (1), Harry Robinson (2), Jack Stone (1) and Tom Berry (2).

None of these were opponents of great account, but they showed Teddy to be a fast hitter and destructive puncher. Within a year, with Phil Scott campaigning in America, they came to the conclusion that Teddy's future lay on the other side of the Atlantic. As Ma had theatrical engagements to fulfil in Europe, Pa accompanied Teddy to the United States where he soon found it was highly necessary to engage an American manager. Ike Dorgan took the job, and set the youngster away to a flying start with a five rounds win over Pietro Corri in New York.

The American fans liked Sandwina, especially those of German origin, but Dorgan overplayed his hand by putting Teddy in with the giant Norwegian, Otto von Porat, who was also on the trail of fame and fortune. Both attempted to win in quick time, and Porat got there first, his right hand (delivering the hardest punch Sandwina had encountered to date) winning by a knockout in round two.

Pa was aghast, and wondered how Kati would take the news. Teddy's pride was hurt as well as his chin. But Mr Dorgan reminded him that Jack Dempsey had once been knocked cold in one round – and see what happened to him! They brightened up considerably after that and in his next six bouts, fought in New York and Boston, Sandwina came out with four wins, one cut-eye stoppage, and one third-round disqualification for an alleged low blow.

With his six-month labour permit expiring, and Kati getting lonely, they returned to London, being met off the boat by Messrs Berliner and Littlestone, who hastily matched Teddy for their next Sunday matinee. With skilful pairing and expert publicity, Sandwina once again became the idol of the East End. In the short space of seven months he had fifteen contests, winning all but one of them inside the distance. Most of the fights took place at Premierland, with the majority of the leading heavyweight contenders as his victims; there was a big clamour that Teddy should now meet Phil Scott.

The British champion had come back from the States where, after a shocking start, he had regained lost ground and now stood out as the foremost challenger for the world title left vacant by Gene Tunney's retirement. Phil was risking a lot in taking on the young German-American, for defeat would ruin his place in the ratings, but Harry Jacobs, the current Albert Hall promoter, dangled such a pot of gold before his eyes that any hesitation was short-lived.

There were more of Sandwina's supporters in the South Kensington arena than there were followers of Scott, and Kati beamed broadly on her neighbours as she sat in the second row of the ringside seats, Max being up in the corner with her wonderful son. Scott had the longest left arm in the business and knew how to use it. He was a master at luring opponents into running against this mighty prop and Sandwina was made to measure. Teddy tried all he knew to hang a heavy right on Phil's suspect chin, but all he got for his pains was a bleeding nose.

Somewhere during the fifth round, he happened to look over the ropes and there was his big, strong mum, crying her eyes out, tears rolling uncontrolled down her cheeks as she watched his handsome features being cut to ribbons. That made Ted savage. He swarmed into the Englishmen and slammed in a right with all his strength behind it. The wild blow missed Scott's jaw, in fact it hit him in the groin. Down went Phil in a heap and the referee walked out of the ring.

Sandwina's disqualification did not lose him any friends. They thought he was worthy of a second chance and seven weeks later he was matched with Charlie Smith, an awkward heavy from Deptford who was well in line for a crack at Scott's crown. In between times Teddy had scored two more quick wins and was a hot favourite to beat Smith, who was not rated very highly by the critics. But the unorthodox Londoner made a monkey out of his eager young rival. He avoided Sandwina's big punches with ridiculous ease and tantalised him with hits that came out of the blue and which Teddy never saw but only felt.

Six rounds of this and the Strong Woman's son lost his temper. Rushing at his tormentor, he hit Smith well below the belt line and was promptly ruled out. This time the Stewards of the Board of Control decided that Teddy should be punished for his sins. He was fined and suspended for three months, a penalty that caused the Sandwina family to leave England for good.

In America Teddy took up where he had left off, but after a good run of successes over second-rate heavies, he came up against that roly-poly of the ring, Tony Galento, in his own home-town of Newark. The New Jersey bar-tender was a mere up-and-comer in those days and had not taken to prodigious beer drinking as part of his training. Even so, he was too rough and tough for Sandwina, who was hammered into submission inside two rounds.

There wasn't much more after that. A year of fighting among the nonentities, then a quick knockout defeat by Primo Carnera and that was enough for Kati. Teddy was 23 then and still very much under her influence. She looked her son in the eye and shook her handsome head. He looked back and nodded. Pa Sandwina packed up the boxing kit and made arrangements for the act to become a family affair once again.

9

His Mistress Drank Him under the Table

John L. Sullivan

It was wine as much as women that ruined John L. Sullivan, the last of the bare-knuckle champions. Up to the time of winning the title, the big, blustering Boston Strong Boy avoided hard liquour for the simple reason that he couldn't afford it, but he liked his beer and this brought about his first clash with the womenfolk who came into his life. Born strong and fearless, Sullivan indulged in all the tough sports as a youth and soon became a local hero. He liked demonstrating his exceptional strength by lifting weights and heavy objects, or proving his superiority as a fighter by knocking someone senseless.

One of the most striking girls in Boston was Kate Harkins, a tall brunette of superb build and plenty of will-power. John L. picked her out as the woman he would condescend to marry, but got the cold shoulder in a big way. 'I am a God-fearing person,' she told him. 'I am opposed to fist fighting and will have nothing to do with a man who drinks alcohol.'

Sullivan explained that he liked fighting and the exciting life of a fighter and that he had to drink a lot of beer to put back the sweat he lost in training. He urged her to marry him and promised that he would make her proud of him. But Kate was adamant. He had to give up both his favourite pastimes if he wished her to become his wife. He gave her a paralysing glare and walked out of her house and into the nearest saloon.

Then he met attractive Annie Bates, a high-kicker in a Solly Square vaudeville show. She was young, pretty and shapely, and fell for the handsome moustachioed young man who waited for her at the stage door. John's courting was fast and furious and they were married in a South Boston Catholic Church. But it did not last. The fighter spent too much time with his men friends, Annie could not keep pace with his drinking, and there were violent quarrels.

They had not been wed long before Sullivan went off to Mississippi City to fight Paddy Ryan for the American heavyweight championship. He left his wife at home and after winning the title never returned to her. Ryan was beaten in nine rounds that lasted only eleven minutes. He took terrific punishment from the mighty bare-knuckled rights that Sullivan crashed into his face.

With his opponent helpless and bleeding on the trampled turf, John L. vaulted over the ropes, ran the hundred yards to his dressing-tent, changed rapidly and took the first train to New Orleans, where there were sportsmen, beautiful women and oceans of champagne to welcome the new champion. From now on life was indeed rosy for Sullivan. His pockets were full of money, he could treat and be treated all day and every day. He only went to bed when totally incapable of drinking any more.

All America wanted to see the great John L., and it was the ambition of many men merely to shake his mighty right hand or feel his bulging biceps. Not a few women also enjoyed that privilege, among them being Ann Livingston, a blonde and beautiful actress who specialised in boy parts. Her ample proportions took the champion's eye at first glance.

To his great joy he found her a woman of the world, fully prepared to live his kind of boisterous life. She didn't mind his drinking – in fact, she encouraged it and more than once drank him under the table, a feat that few, if any, men could achieve. When Sullivan came to London in 1887 she travelled with him, but never flaunted herself in his company, keeping in the background, but nevertheless being a great influence.

There was to be a fight with Charley Mitchell at Chantilly in France; Ann crossed the Channel with John L. Determined to be at the ringside, she stuffed herself into a man's suit and stood by the ropes, guarded by two 'whips', to see her hero do battle with the British champion. She had to stand for a long time, as the fight went 39 rounds that lasted three hours and ten minutes. The lighter man by 35 pounds, Mitchell put up a game battle, having the satisfaction of drawing blood from the American's nose with a stiff left jab in the eighth round.

John L. tried his hardest to knock out the cocky Britisher. He did floor him once, but Charley jumped up, stuck out his tongue and defied the Boston Strong Boy to do it again. Halfway through the contest it started to rain and the fighters were soon churning up the mud as they rampaged over the worn grass. Then, when dusk was falling and neither of them looked like surrendering, the referee stopped the exchanges and declared a 'draw'.

Sullivan and Miss Livingston returned to America and continued their roistering. They drank happily, they quarrelled, but they stuck together. More than once they came to blows and on one occasion he sent her staggering with a slap on the face. Quick as a flash she picked up a champagne bottle and cracked him over the head. Down went the champion and Annie could claim that she had been the first person in the world to knock him out.

Like most successful men, Sullivan had enemies and the chief of these was Richard K. Fox, owner and publisher of the celebrated *Police Gazette*, a lurid sporting journal that patronised the Prize Ring. John L. had publicly insulted Mr Fox, who vowed he would find someone to lick the blustering Bostonian. At length he produced Jake Kilrain, a tough 200-pound Irishman, who was undefeated in nine years of bare-knuckle bruising.

Fox announced his readiness to back Kilrain for a substantial side-stake and Sullivan's friends were eager to do business. But when they sought out the champion and told him about the match, they found him a very sick man. His fine physique had broken down under the strain of continual abuse, and he had been seriously ill for months. The challenge by Kilrain could not be ignored, however, so they hired William Muldoon, a noted physical culturist, to get John L. into shape.

Five thousand dollars were posted and the weakened Sullivan was hustled off to Muldoon's training camp. All liquor was barred, John had to undergo a gruelling preparation and Ann Livingston found herself banned from the champion's presence. The lady was highly indignant. She defied Muldoon by turning up one day and taking Sullivan off on a drinking joust when the trainer's back was turned, but the spree was short-lived.

Muldoon tracked the pair to the private bar of the nearest saloon and there was a noisy showdown. The champion was ready to deal with his trainer by force, but Muldoon, a great wrestler in his youth, swept John L. off his feet, threw him on the sawdust floor, applied a half-nelson, and threatened to break his arm if he did not tell Miss Livingston to beat it and also promise to return to the training camp and behave himself.

It was a miracle the way Muldoon licked the dissipated champion into fighting condition. He turned a flabby, savagely abused, physique into something approaching the old war-horse. Sullivan's backers had agreed to pay Muldoon ten thousand dollars if he got John L. into the ring against Kilrain in reasonable shape. Big Bill told them he would not take the money if the champion lost.

The title fight took place at Richburg, Mississippi, on the estate of a timber merchant named Charles Rich. All through the night labourers worked to put up the seating and erect the ring and at dawn on 8 July 1889, Kilrain and Sullivan climbed over the ropes. Every effort had been made to see that Ann Livingston was kept away, but there she was, dressed as a man, surrounded by a tough bodyguard. And for over two hours she screamed encouragement at her lover, while Sullivan fought the toughest battle of his life.

Hard as nails, well trained and hating Sullivan's guts, Kilrain tried his utmost to win the championship, but John L., his ears ringing with Ann's yells and Muldoon's threats each time he got back to his corner, fought on doggedly, ending each round by either throwing the Irishman or knocking him down.

As the fight went on so the temperature mounted until it registered 100 degrees. Kilrain suffered most in the intense heat and took the heaviest punishment. Time after time he had to be dragged to his corner, and during the 75th round a ringside physician told Jake's chief second to throw in the towel to save a game man from being killed.

Sullivan's victory made him a national hero and he lived like a prince wherever he went. He was now mixing in higher society and had no more time for Miss Livingston. Quite abruptly he dismissed her from his life, but it was about five years too late. With no chance of returning to the stage, she opened a boarding house, but it was an unsuccessful venture, mainly because she drank away the profits. In a few years she had died and John L. sent a huge wreath to her funeral.

Parting with her had not changed his mode of living. The hard drinking and the loose living continued and for three years he went the pace without going near a gymnasium or putting up his fists in serious combat. Then he agreed to defend his championship against James J. Corbett, a San Franciscan bank clerk eight years his junior. They fought in the main event of a three-day fistic carnival at the Olympic Club in New Orleans on 2 September 1892; opposed by a man eight years his junior and at the peak of physical fitness, Sullivan was soundly thrashed and knocked out in 21 rounds.

He was still only 34, but an old man in health, his body a mockery of the fine physical machine it had once been. There was never any question of a comeback; gradually the flow of money dried up and his style of living changed accordingly. In 1910 he married his old sweetheart, Kate Harkins. For several years they toured the States lecturing on the evils of strong drink, pointing to himself as a striking example.

10

Ma's Help
Shortened his Career

Tommy Jackson

It would have been better for Tommy Jackson, the young coloured heavyweight from Far Rockaway, New York, if his mother had stuck to her original ideas about boxing. When she first heard that her youngest and favourite son was planning to be a fighter, she slapped him across the ear with a heavy hand and told him to forget it. But when he disobeyed her and began bringing home a fistful of dollar bills from his ring earnings, she changed her mind.

You couldn't blame her. When her husband died, Mrs Georgia Jackson found herself with a brood of eight, four girls and four boys, and little prospect of being able to support them in the Southern town of Sparta, Georgia. So she brought the family to New York and hustled them through a meagre schooling and into jobs as fast as possible. All except Tommy. She sent him to school, but more often than not he never got there, and the educational inspectors never came looking for him, because none of the teachers ever complained about his absence.

Tommy hadn't a head for learning and classrooms gave him claustrophobia. He liked to run round the streets, climb up the sides of houses and roam about over the rooftops. Sometimes he fell off, but apart from a broken wrist on one occasion, he was rarely hurt, and in any case, seemed impervious to pain. When school-leaving age came, young Jackson could not read or write. But he was chock-full of energy, could run like a hare, climb like a monkey and swarm over an opponent like an electrified octopus.

A patrolman, Frank Leonetti, moving in to break up a street

fight, watched in amazement at Tommy's whirlwind way of scrapping. He did not think it possible that anyone could punch so fast and keep it up for so long. He separated Jackson from his victim, another coloured boy, and marched Tommy off to the police station. He did not charge him; instead he took the boy into the gymnasium and showed him round. Tommy's eyes opened wide in wonderment at the training appliances, the ring and the wrestling mat. To a youngster of his boundless energy it was paradise.

When he was told he could come and be taught how to box, young Jackson came every day of the week. That was when his mother struck her decisive blow against boxing, but it did not stop Tommy. He pushed his delivery truck around the Long Island streets during the day and rushed into the gymnasium every evening. Very often they had to put out the lights and threaten to lock him in before he could be induced to go home.

Leonetti gave up trying to teach Jackson to box after the first lesson. From then on he let him go his own sweet unscientific way and Jackson ploughed through the amateurs, beating boys far more talented than himself by the simple process of bewildering them with a ceaseless flood of flaying fists. His mentor had ideas about a professional career. He brought in Lippe Breidart, a transport executive, as fight manager and Sammy Golden, a veteran boxer, as trainer. They thought they had a goldmine in Tommy, but Mrs Jackson was so dead against the idea that they had to wait until he was 21 before launching him in the paid ranks.

By this time Jackson stood 6ft 3in., weighed just under 200 pounds and had a reach of 80 inches. He couldn't punch properly, had no idea of timing, was always falling over his own feet and knew absolutely nothing about ring-craft. He dabbed, clubbed, thumped and flapped in perpetual motion, introducing his 'kangaroo' punch, an uppercut landed with both fists simultaneously, which made the fistic professors shudder. Tommy had no defence beyond his ceaseless attacking, but his head was hard and his chin rocklike. Most of his early opponents just caved in under his avalanche of leather, and in two years Jackson had 12 wins in 14 bouts with one drawn.

For his first main event they put Jackson into Madison Square Garden with Rex Layne, a tough ring-worn heavy, but still a danger to most men below the top. Tommy hustled him to a state of exhaustion inside six rounds and did it in such overwhelming style that next morning he found himself named 'The Hurricane'. Some of the boxing writers thought that at the way he was going he might earn himself a shot at the heavyweight championship.

His pay packet for a quick night's work, plus the colourful publicity, caused Mrs Jackson to change her mind. After all, her Tommy was in the news, everyone was talking about him and the big roll he had brought home nicely filled out the usually sucked-in sides of her handbag. She entertained his trio of sponsors who were splitting a big proportion of his earnings three ways. They came very unwillingly and left very thought-fully, Ma having explained that in future she would be personally responsible for her son's erratic behaviour, both in and out of the ring. 'He always does what I say,' she announced, pounding one beefy fist into the other. 'You say what you want him to do and I'll see that he does it.'

She visited the promoter's office when the contracts were signed, she sat in a seat as close to his corner as she could get and never missed the pay-out ceremony when Tommy picked up his purses. They taught Jackson how to sign a cheque and count his money, but they couldn't teach him how to box or to avoid getting hit. It did not seem necessary until the night the Cuban Giant, Nino Valdes, had him down three times in the second round and the referee stopped it. Tommy wasn't hurt – or at least showed no signs of it – but there was a new Boxing Commission ruling that three knockdowns in a single round called for a stoppage and this had been enforced.

Naturally, Jackson, his mentors and Ma protested loud and long, overlooking the fact that a stiff puncher, hitting off the right foot with good timing could drop him easily despite his 'iron chin'. To demonstrate his disapproval of the verdict and to prove he would have been fully capable of continuing,

Tommy ran round the Madison Square Garden block – a matter of a quarter-mile – twelve times.

They gave him a few suckers after that, then he beat such name fighters as Jimmy Slade, Ezzard Charles, Bob Baker and Johnny Williams, the former British champion, and was nominated to fight Floyd Patterson in an eliminator for the world title left vacant by the retirement of Rocky Marciano. Jackson was favoured to win and he gave his fellow-townee the hardest fight of his so-far triumphant career. The fans roared as Tommy flailed away at Floyd and the referee thought he had done enough to win, but was overruled by the judges who voted for Patterson.

There had to be a re-match and they met 13 months later. By now Floyd had won the championship by knocking out Archie Moore and the return with Tommy was his first title defence. Meanwhile Jackson had gone his haywire way, participating in only two bouts, both of which went the distance, suggesting that the 'Hurricane' had begun to blow itself out. He still flogged himself in training, doing his roadwork by the hour instead of the mile, pounding away at the big bag in long sessions, and swarming over his sparring-partners in a riot of whirling, aimless arms.

Someone told Ma Jackson that he was preferring hot-dogs to steaks and stuffing himself with soft drinks and ice cream, so she moved into camp and took over the cooking. Her son did not like this interference with his diet. He sulked, he ran away, he nearly got himself drowned. But his mother would not budge and Tommy got peeved. That is no way for a fighter to train for a championship contest.

Jackson's only asset was his whirlwind style, and this proved no problem to Patterson this time. Floyd drilled through his erratic defence with scientific precision and Tommy took a shameful hiding. Dropped in the first round from a sizzling right to the chin, he was down again in the second, but foolishly got up at 'two'. After that the 'Hurricane' became the mildest of zephyrs and the champion hit him at will.

Tommy could only fight in flurries now and Patterson treated his attacks with disdain. Yet Jackson kept coming out, and no one in his corner tried to stop him. Another cracking right hook sent Tommy sprawling in the ninth round. He looked done, but scrambled to his feet at 'four', and now his efforts to fight back were so pathetic that the fans screamed at the referee to stop it. Ruby Goldstein obliged halfway through the tenth and Jackson was in such a bad way that the doctor had him removed to hospital where it was found necessary to detain him. Ma and his managers stayed behind to look after the 62,000 dollars that were Tommy's share of the gate.

Next day the champion and his wife called at the hospital to enquire after Jackson, but were informed that he had discharged himself. Right there his mother should have insisted that he said goodbye to boxing. He had got as far as he would ever get, he was 26 and to suffer another bad beating might be dangerous.

Yet he was back in the ring three months later, meeting talented Eddie Machen at San Francisco in a 12-round fight labelled as a world title eliminator. It was a repetition of the Patterson fight. Jackson made a brief showing until floored by a snappy right to the chin in the opening round. After that it was scientific slaughter with the game – too game – Tommy collapsing in his corner at the end of the tenth and being unable to come out for the next.

This time they locked the dressing-room door and worked over him until he was fit enough to leave the arena. Now it was indeed the end, even Ma could see that. Two years later he did attempt a comeback, and although he won three bouts out in the sticks, the majority of the Boxing Commissions refused to grant him a licence. With great reluctance Tommy was forced to call it a day.

11

He Owed Everything to his Missus

George Cook

The toughest fighter I ever knew was 'Evergreen' George Cook, the Australian lumberjack who twice fought his way round the world in a turbulent career that started when he was eighteen and ended when he was forty. Apart from being heavyweight champion of Australia, Cook never won another title, yet he crossed gloves with the best men of his day and destroyed the hopes of many an ambitious young fighter – a wonderful record for a man handicapped by lack of height, yet he told me more than once: 'I owe everything to my missus. I couldn't get along without her.'

He met her soon after he came to London in 1921. She was a young war widow and was so attracted to the quiet and reserved 23-year old Australian boxer that she decided to marry him. They lived at St. John's Wood, and each morning, including Sundays, George would get up at six and run round nearby Regent's Park – and his bath and his breakfast would be ready on his return. Mid-morning he would set off for the gymnasium, his kit washed and neatly packed by his loyal wife. But she would never go to see him fight and would sit by the window awaiting his homecoming, ready to administer to his bruises and console him in the event of defeat.

Most times, George had to give away considerable height and bulk, yet he never turned down a contest and often entered the ring without a ghost of a chance according to the experts. He fooled them many times. Twice he fought big Frank Goddard, who towered over him and carried a punch like the kick of a mule. Cook won both contests on points after 20 hard-hitting rounds, and was so knocked-about on the second occasion that one of his pals took him to his front door, propped the groggy Australian up in the porch, rang the bell and fled.

Mrs Cook then looked tearfully at his swollen eyes, lumpy chin and mashed lips: 'There must be something wrong with your guard,' she opined, and although it hurt to grin, George grinned. 'It's no laughing matter,' said his wife. 'Just look at you, anyone would think you had been run over. The next time you have a work-out, I'm coming to see it.' 'That'll be tomorrow,' answered Cook. 'Let's go to bed.'

From that time onwards she had a partnership in her husband's boxing career. She studied diet and cooked his meals. Although George had an official manager, she had a big say in every move he made. She watched other boxers in action and made suggestions whereby her husband could tighten up his defence, improve his footwork and get the maximum power behind his punches.

Some trainers sneered at having a woman in the gym, but George thrived on it. Having her around to watch his work-outs gave him great comfort and encouragement. His first bout under his wife's guidance was with Paolino Uzcudun, a tough Spaniard who carried a murderous punch, was unbeaten, and outweighed the Australian by over a stone.

Everyone felt sorry for Cook, yet he astounded them all by winning handsomely on points and coming out without a scratch. True, George had taken a few heavy clouts, but his face was unmarked. 'It's all thanks to you,' he told his wife, and she replied: 'Well, it's supposed to be the Art of Self-Defence, isn't it ?'

Fights came with frequency after that. Cook did not win them all, but except for the time when he was knocked out by famous Georges Carpentier, he was always on his feet at the finish and looking as though he could manage another fifteen or twenty rounds without any trouble. He fought Italians, Dutchmen, Germans, Swedes, Frenchman, Spaniards and any Britisher who cared to swap punches. By 1925, after licking Tom Heeney, the tough-as-teak New Zealander, an offer came for a series of bouts in Boston.

'Take it,' urged Mrs Cook. 'You're guaranteed six well-paid contests in five months. When you come back we'll open a flower shop.' 'Aint' you coming? ' asked George. 'We've got to be sensible about this,' she argued. 'Keeping me will eat too deep into the profits. You can manage without me for a little while.' So off he set for America, but as soon as they reached Cherbourg, he was so depressed he sent an S.O.S. telegram imploring her to follow on the next boat.

They stayed eighteen months, and if George lost more contests than he won, at least he was being well paid for it. The tour finished in San Francisco just before Christmas and walking round the docks they saw a liner due to leave for Australia in a day or two. 'Let's go,' suggested Mrs Cook. They went and George engaged in a few bouts to pay their expenses during the visit home, after which they decided to come back to London, dropping off in Johannesburg for a couple of contests with the South African champion, Johnny Squires.

Back in London the Cooks found a new menace had arisen in the heavyweight ranks. Teddy Sandwina, the young German-American had been knocking the local big boys about, left, right and centre. His backers welcomed the arrival of the veteran Aussie as another piece of cannon-fodder. 'Fight him? Of course George will fight him,' announced Mrs Cook when Charlie Cochran's matchmaker approached her. It was to be a supporting contest to the world's middleweight title fight between Mickey Walker and Tommy Milligan at Olympia.

It was five to one against Cook, but George messed the youngster about so much, ripped open his right eye, and had him in such a bewildered state that the referee stopped the contest in round three. Sandwina wasn't satisfied, so Cook met him again, this time at the Blackfriars Ring, and gave him a boxing lesson for fifteen rounds to win by a wide points margin.

Promoters in Berlin, Milan and Rome had local talent they hoped to advance at Cook's expense and if George did not get the verdict each time, he secured a drawn decision, which amounted to the same thing. Then, having proved himself a real nuisance and his name obnoxious to managers with young heavies, George set off with his wife, and daughter Julie, on another world tour. He was away two years, during whch he boxed in most of the American big-fight cities, went to Brazil and Canada, and wound up by touring Australia and New Zealand again.

Back in England they had to review the situation. George was 34 but still full of fight; his wife had an eleven-year-old daughter to look after, besides the flower shop she now opened. They appointed Charlie Rose, a newspaper man with an Australian background, to look after George's future ring activities. But after sitting in his Fetter Lane office for a month without an enquiry coming through, Rose began to wonder if indeed Cook had any future.

Luckily for them, the boxing fans in Leicester had a lust for heavyweights and, searching round for anyone who could stay a few rounds with the French champion, Maurice Griselle, someone suggested the sawn-off Australian. 'George will be there at the finish,' they assured the promoter; so he was, the winner on a foul struck by the frustrated foreigner in round twelve.

Cook was back in business, and did so well in subsequent fights that promoter Jeff Dickson decided to put him in with Primo Carnera. The giant Italian topped George by twelve inches and outweighed him by five stones; the fight scribes rushed round to Mrs Cook *en masse*. 'What's the panic?' she asked. They wanted to know if she had ever seen Carnera. 'Of course, I have,' she told them. 'Didn't George make a monkey out of him in Cleveland, Ohio, two years ago. He'd have stopped him if he hadn't been getting over a touch of influenza.' She turned away to attend to a customer. Cook did not win, but he fought gamely until Carnera pounded him down in the fourth round and George was too tired to get up in time to beat the count.

Down in Cardiff, bookmaker Jimmy Jones turned promoter and staged a match between Jack Petersen, the idol of Welsh fans, and Evergreen George, at Ninian Park. Although Cook had an experienced trainer, his wife always went with him to his dressing-room as soon as they got to the arena. Tiny, petitite, blonde, wearing horned-rimmed glasses, she would make sure he had everything he would require in the ring, give any advice she thought fit, kiss him, wish him good luck, and then go and sit at the ringside, watching the minor contests and awaiting the arrival of her husband in the main event of the show. She was sitting with Charlie Rose when the promoter joined them. 'How long do you think the old fellow will last?' he asked the manager, who answered that George would be there at the finish. The Welshman roared with laughter and told him he was crazy. That was too much for Mrs Cook. 'Excuse me, Mr Jones,' she snapped, 'but you're talking about my husband. If you think Petersen will stop George in a few rounds, it is you who's crazy.'

She was right. Cook kept the young Cardiff man up on his toes for the full fifteen rounds and there could not have been a lot in it at the finish when Petersen was declared the winner. They met again eighteen months later when Cook made his second attempt to win the British Empire title. George was 36 then, but again he went the distance, although the margin in Petersen's favour was larger this time.

George badly wanted to win a championship and when Larry Gains, that fine coloured Canadian, was titleholder he was challenged persistently by the Australian for nearly two years. At last they met at Olympia and Mrs Cook, as usual, sat at the ringside, close by her husband's corner. During the intervals she would leave her chair and give George advice from the foot of the steps. He would always look round to let her know he had heard.

It was a tense battle between a stand-up boxer and a rugged infighter and Cook attacked from start to finish. In his eagerness to weaken his taller opponent, George was guilty of grabbing hold of Gains with one hand and pulling him on to savage hooks from the other. He got warned a couple of times for this and at the end of the round his wife called: 'Don't get disqualified, George, I don't mind you losing, but not on a foul.'

Only once did she get excited. Midway through the eighth Cook landed a smashing left hook to the solar plexus and had

Gains in real distress. He rolled along the ropes showing the whites of his eyes and Mrs Cook leapt to her feet. 'After him, George,' she yelled. 'You've got him now, don't give him a chance to get away.'

No man needed more encouragement and gallant Cook tried his utmost to bring the Empire champion down. But Gains was no novice; he had got out of difficulties before, and he got out of this one, using the ring and all his defensive skill to stay clear of further trouble until the bell.

Cook had exhausted himself with this big effort and Gains never gave him another such opportunity. Even so, there were many among the spectators who disagreed with the verdict in Larry's favour, their sympathies being with the veteran warrior who had forced the pace all the way.

When the Board of Control refused to review his boxer's licence in 1939, George was indignant. 'I'm only 40 and got a lot more life in me than some of the heavyweights I see around,' he argued. But they turned him down and Mrs Cook sighed with relief. 'All right,' declared her irrepressible husband, 'then I'll join the National Fire Service. Anything for some action.'

12

Ladies' Man
but No Champion

Jack Doyle

If you are tall, dark and handsome it is generally supposed that the romantic side of your life will be highly successful. It can also be a considerable asset in the realms of entertainment and sport. If, in addition, you happen to possess a power-packed punch in your right hand, the way should be pretty clear for a fabulous career as a professional boxer, especially if you are heavyweight in size.

Jack Doyle, the former Irish Guardsman, had all these advantageous qualities, in fact, his passport into the prize ring was gilt-edged. Yet, he failed to win a championship and faded out of the Fight Game after only a score of contests stretched over seven years.

Looking at his short record, it is hard to believe that so much sensation and drama was packed into it. Doyle wasn't wholly to blame. He was spoiled by his manager, who for publicity purposes introduced his 18-year-old discovery into places, and among society, far removed from the humble circumstances into which the young Irishman had been born.

There was nothing glamorous about the thatched cottage with the earthen floor in which his family lived at Queenstown, just outside Cork. It was so low that when Jack was in his early 'teens, he could barely stand up in it without cracking his head on the roof. Of course, even as a youth he stood 5ft 11in. and scaled 180 pounds – a tough, strong youngster, who got work as a bricklayer's labourer after school hours in order to add to the household budget.

Life was extremely dull around Queenstown, and Doyle envied those who had the money to spend on good food and fun. So at sixteen he advanced his age by two years and enlisted in the Irish Guards. Six months' training at Caterham Barracks, and he was sent to Windsor, where he was put into the battalion boxing championships without being asked whether he knew how to box or even if he wanted to learn about the Noble Art. He looked big enough to beat anybody, but knew nothing of the finer points of fighting. Not that this was necessary in the type of battling his soldier opponents could provide. Jack merely wound up his big right arm and let it go with lusty abandon. He won most of his bouts in the opening round.

In Windsor there was the Star and Garter, a hostelry that catered for boxers who needed a long spell of training. There was a well-equipped gymnasium attached to the premises, and Doyle would go along in his spare time and watch the sparring. On one occasion Len Harvey was preparing for an important fight and the young Irishman looked on eagerly, even suggesting to the British champion that he might be allowed to have a round or two. A genial and obliging character, Harvey amused himself as Jack tried hard to get through his immaculate guard with one of his swinging punches, being content to tap the youngster on the nose now and again just to let him know who was guvnor. When the work-out ended and Doyle had gone back to barracks, Len went to the telephone and told Dan Sullivan that if he was short of a heavyweight there was one to be picked up for the asking.

Sullivan, who managed the Ring at Blackfriars besides a stable of fighters, came and watched the young Irishman in action. Straight away he bought Doyle out of the Guards and started him off on a professional career. Jack was $18\frac{1}{2}$ then, and before his twentieth birthday he was fighting for the British heavyweight title with a guaranteed purse of £3,000 for his services. Up to that point he had won all his ten contests, not one of which had gone more than two rounds. He was the talk of the town, the biggest box-office attraction the Fight Game had known for a long time. His championship contest with Jack Petersen, known as the Welsh Tiger, packed out the White City Stadium with fifty thousand excited fans.

Jack was confident he could wipe the ring floor with the talented Welshman; his army of followers prophesied that the fight would end in a couple of rounds. They were right, but not as they imagined. Irish Jack swarmed over Welsh Jack and became so excited he completely forgot that there were a set of rules to be observed. His wild blows soon earned him a caution from the referee, but Doyle paid no heed. In his anxiety to win in sensational style, he punched low more than once, and midway through the second round found himself disqualified.

The Irishman could not believe it when the Board of Control impounded his purse and suspended him for six months. Actually he stayed out of the ring for two years except for a solitary appearance when he scored a one-round knockout victory over Frank Borrington. That long spell of inactivity was Doyle's ruin, because he found that his personality and good looks, plus his colourful, if brief, ring appearances, were sufficient to bring him the best things in life – for free.

The time he had used to spend in preparing for a contest was now devoted to cocktail parties and social engagements. The dim lights of the night clubs were even more attractive than the glare of the ring lights. The charms of the fair sex were far more agreeable than the rough-and-ready company of the training camps. Instead of spending his mornings in the gymnasium, he stayed in bed recovering from the pleasures of the night before.

Promoters still wanted his services and Jack kept promising himself that he would return to the punching profession at any moment. But he always had second thoughts about it, and when in 1935 he decided to go to America, no one could have cared less. Yet Doyle was still only 21 and a serious attempt to make a comeback might have proved successful. He got to New York, quickly found a backer and announced that he had arrived for the sole purpose of winning the world's title. His fighting record of 13 fights, which included twelve knockout wins and that single loss because of an alleged foul, looked most impressive and plans were soon made to give him an opportunity to show his fistic paces in Madison Square Garden itself.

It was the chance of a lifetime, but Doyle did not intend to be rushed into a return to the ring. First he insisted on going to Hollywood where he felt he might find a better locale for his talents. For Jack had a pleasing singing voice and sufficient blarney on his tongue to get him into show business. He also imagined he might meet with success as a lady-killer among the glamorous beauties of the film city. He was right. Within a week he had encountered Judith Allen, a dazzling starlet who had recently divorced herself from heavyweight wrestling champion, Bud Sonnenberg.

Despite urgent requests from New York to come back and commence preparation for his American debut in return for the funds that had been advanced to him for his Hollywood trip, Doyle lingered on in the company of the lovely Miss Allen, finally taking her off to Mexico where he married her in a register office at Agua Caliente. A lengthy honeymoon followed as a matter of course, but eventually the Doyles arrived in New York where they lived in lavish splendour until the Irishman was forced to fight because of acute shortness of money.

Jack's American debut took place at the Dychman Oval in Brooklyn and 7,000 curious fans saw him knock out their local hero, Phil Donato, with one mighty right to the chin. A fortnight later, Bob Norton went out with a bang in similar fashion, then Doyle journeyed to Newark in New Jersey and disposed of Jack Redmond, but took four rounds in which to do it. Then came the real test, a match with Buddy Baer in the Garden. Younger brother to the renowned Maxie, he was taller than Doyle and outweighed him by 25 pounds. But he was notoriously slow and had he been as fit as he should have been, Jack might have overcome these handicaps.

He started off by tossing a terrific right at Buddy that caught him on the side of the head and sent him staggering. Doyle blew a kiss to Judith, who was sitting at the ringside, and when he looked back at his opponent, Baer was bearing down on him full of vengeance. With a savage right swing, he caught the

Irishman well below the belt-line and Doyle went down in a heap. Jack knew that he was boxing under no-foul conditions and that if he stayed on the canvas he would be counted out. So he struggled to his feet to beat the timekeeper, but much of the fight had been knocked out of him. Three times he landed his pet punch on Buddy's chin and each time Baer recoiled but kept his blance. Another tremendous right from the American giant crashed against Jack's jaw and he slithered to the canvas. Up at the count of 'three', another crumpled him up for five seconds. Gamely he got to his feet once more, but the referee had seen enough. He waved the dazed Doyle back to his corner and raised his rival's hand as the winner.

That one-round defeat put paid to Jack's American adventures, but only so far as the ring was concerned. An offer came from London for a fight with Tommy Farr, so Jack left his Judy and returned home. Here he ignored another wonderful chance to make good as a boxer. Instead of signing a contract to fight, he entered into a social whirl that brought him into contact with Mrs Delphine Dodge-Godde, the motor car millionairess. Dancing with her and sharing her champagne was far more pleasant than swapping punches and, despite all the lucrative offers, Jack just beamed at promoters and told them not to be impatient.

They waited a year and a half, during which time his association with Delphine earned him, not surprisingly, considerable trouble from Judith, who threatened all sorts of things in retaliation. Doyle hastened back to the U.S.A., getting entangled with Libby Holman, an American torch dancer, en route. Before he had time to soothe down his wife, Mrs Dodge-Godde arrived on his trail, whereupon Judith sued her for two million dollars, alleging that she had bought her husband's affections. Jack denied the charge, but his wife went ahead and obtained a divorce, but whether she got her two million is not known. Delphine did not particularly want to become Mrs Doyle No. 2, and just when he was wondering where next to turn, the Irishman received an invitation from Arthur Elvin to box at Wembley Arena.

No other fighter in ring history was given more opportunities to prove himself, but Doyle made a complete hash of his return to the ring by being disqualified in the very first round. He floored his opponent, Alf Robinson, with a mighty clout to the head, then proceeded to batter him while down, being immediately ruled out and leaving the ring to a storm of booing. But all that was forgotten and forgiven when a month later, he was matched with Harry Staal at Earl's Court and a packed house saw him beat down the stolid Dutchman in six rounds.

Next they imported the notorious King Levinsky as an opponent for Jack at Wembley Arena, in a supporting bout to a world's flyweight championship match between Benny Lynch and Small Montana from the Philippines. The former Chicago fish-porter was past his best, but still a tough swinger likely to cause the erratic Doyle a lot of trouble. All the available tickets were snapped up weeks beforehand, and it is safe to say that more came to see the big boys as did those who were interested in the little men. They were entitled to a real punch-up, instead they sat through the full ten rounds and gaped as the Irishman waltzed round his cumbersome rival, planting a long left into his battered features, while the King swung wildly and in vain.

The reason for this unusually subdued performance on the Irishman's part was simple. An anonymous sportsman, eager that Doyle should develop into a class performer, had offered him a pound note for every straight left he landed during the contest and money-minded Jack was out to earn every penny possible. He won on points, but seventeen months went by before he treated the fans to another performance. This time promoter Sydney Hulls thought up a match between the unpredictable Irishman and Eddie Phillips, from Bow, who at one time had been the British light-heavyweight champion.

Ten thousand eager spectators packed into Harringay Arena and Doyle knew they were there. A few minutes before the fight was due to go on he sent for the promoter and demanded more money than had been previously agreed. When told he could go to hell, Jack started to divest himself of his fighting gear. 'In that case, Sydney my bhoy, Oi'll be going home.' He meant it, or at least Hulls thought he meant it. A pen was found, a cheque book produced, but even then Doyle was not satisfied. 'Oi'll be taking some of it in cash,' he said – and got it.

The promoter got very poor return for his money. Jack spent the first round trying to land a big punch on the stylish Phillips and in the second rushed across the ring to aim a mighty blow at the Londoner's chin. Phillips had all the time in the world to dodge the punch and Doyle's 210 pounds went hurtling over the ropes to land him on the floor behind the row of crouching pressmen. He got up and stood there while the timekeeper counted him out with the assistance of Sam Russell, Phillips' manager, who made sure that Jack heard every second.

Early next morning, as soon as the banks were open, Doyle cashed his cheque and, being anxious to escape Mr Hulls' wrath, took flight to America. But not to fight. He thought there might be further romantic adventures in Hollywood and made his way there, lingering in Chicago to have an affair with Betty Liza Strathmore, a 22-year-old dancing instructor, who threatened to poison herself if he left her, and dallying with dancer Elinor Troy in Los Angeles before coming to rest in the film city.

He had not been there very long before he was captivated by the charms, or she with his, of the lovely Mexican film star, Movita Castenada. She was an established actress under her first name, her initial success being as one of the native wives in *Mutiny on the Bounty*. In next to no time they were married and conjuring up a successful singing act. When this began to lose its lustre in America, they brought it to London and Doyle could not have chosen a more appropriate moment.

A big open-air show was being planned for the White City Stadium, with Len Harvey and Jock McAvoy topping the bill in a bout advertised as for the light-heavyweight championship of the world, a title that had just been vacated by John Henry Lewis because of eyesight trouble. The promoters offered Jack two thousand pounds to fight a return contest with Eddie Phillips in chief support.

No one knows exactly how many people were there that

July night of 1939. All roads to the arena were blocked hours before the main event was staged, barriers were broken down by the milling fans, and whether they poured in to see Harvey and McAvoy fight for the fourth time, or if they were drawn at the prospect of seeing more fireworks from Doyle and Phillips, is anyone's guess. As it happens those who came because the spectacular Irishman was on the programme had their fill of drama, even if it was very short-lived.

Harvey had no sooner been awarded a narrow points win over his aggressive challenger, than Doyle and Phillips came into the ring. The excitement was intense and the impatient fans could barely wait for the starting gong. As soon as it sounded Doyle dashed at Phillips and lashed out with his big right. It landed, Eddie sat down, and a mighty roar rocked the Stadium. The Londoner scrambled to his feet only to be bowled over again by another furious charge from the big Irishman. Once more Phillips touched the canvas and while he located his corner and got the signal to rise, Jack walked round the ring, his chest puffed out, ready to show all and sundry that he was back with a bang.

He was! Phillips climbed up, took guard and waited for the next assault. In tore Doyle, leading with his dimpled chin; he met a stiff straight left flush on the point. Down he went like a felled tree. He struck the canvas with the back of his head and lay perfectly still, his hands by his sides, and did not move a muscle while the timekeeper beat out the full count. It was his last fight in the ring, but not his last domestic battle. He and his temperamental Movita had numerous wars, both public and in private, until one day she packed her bags and walked out, leaving the devil-may-care Doyle to his own devices.

13

His Wife was
his Sparring-partner

Jimmy Wilde

What made Jimmy Wilde one of the greatest flyweight champions the world has ever seen was probably his wife's strong objection to boxing. Her father, Dai Davies, was one of the typical Welsh mountain fighters of the time and through her mother she acquired an inborn dislike for fisticuffs. Small wonder, therefore, that she turned up her nose at the diminutive Jimmy when he first put in an appearance at her home.

Wilde was fifteen then and had been working in the coal mines near Tylorstown in South Wales for over two years. He was passionately fond of boxing, no doubt because of his small size, and as soon as he learned that famous Dai Davies was in the same pit as himself, he lost no time in getting himself engaged as helper.

Weighing little more than 84 pounds, Jimmy was so skinny he could have got a job in a freak show as a living skeleton at any fairground. Instead, he was always climbing into the ring of the boxing booth that opened every Saturday night on a vacant piece of ground in the neighbourhood. There he would dispose of opponent after opponent, usually men much bigger than himself, with the extraordinary knockout power contained in his whipcord muscles.

These had been developed at the coal face, Wilde's tiny figure enabling him to work in the seams too shallow to take a normal-sized man. Jimmy would lie on his side and hew out the black diamonds ahead of him, then scrape them back to his workmate, these being the days when pick and muscle power were the main sources of production. When they broke off for a rest the old fighter would show Jimmy the boxing moves he had used so effectively and successfully in his Sunday morning bare-fist battles of the past.

Most of Wilde's early contests earned him nothing more than a packet of cigarettes, yet he thought about little else but swapping punches and was so keen to improve that Dai took him home for further instruction. Mrs Davies and her daughter 'Lisbeth plainly disapproved, so tutor and pupil had to go into the tiny bedroom for the boxing lessons. Even with the bed and the other furniture pushed aside, there was little available space in a typical Welsh miner's home of those days, but they were not discouraged.

The less space to move in meant concentration on footwork and body shifting, boxing qualities that Jimmy brought to perfection and which eventually took him to the world's title. He absorbed every trick and artifice that his mentor could impart and before long Wilde was known throughout the Rhondda Valley as 'The Tylorstown Terror'.

Meanwhile, he had become very fond of Miss Davies. At eighteen he was drawing full miner's pay, three pounds and ten shillings a fortnight, plus the five bob he got for every booth bout. He felt he could afford to contemplate marriage. One night he boldly popped the question, but was not prepared for the answer. If she accepted him, would he be willing to give up boxing and concentrate on being a miner. It was a simple but firm request and Jimmy just stared at her. Here he was being given the choice of the two things that mattered most in his life. To marry 'Lisbeth or to box. There was no question of doing both so he asked if she would marry him if he promised to stay away from the ring for good.

Miss Davies agreed and Jimmy capitulated. They got married without delay, but when Wilde discovered that he was reduced to a bare sixpence a week pocket money, his thoughts returned to the bright lights of the boxing booth, the roar of the crowd and the cash to be earned for knocking someone over in a round or two. The lure was too great and he broke his marriage vow by visiting the booths and small arenas in places outside of Tylorstown.

Now he had to be careful not to go home with a cut or a

bruise that could not be attributed to the hazardous work in the pits. He had to hit his opponents first and hard enough to put them down and out in quick time in order to return to his wife with unblemished features. And so a phenomenal world-beater was developed, an under-sized fighting machine with the eye of an eagle and the kick of a mule in each glove, plus the ability to avoid punishment that was almost uncanny. No wonder someone named him 'The Ghost with a Hammer in his Hand'.

The best of schemers get found out eventually. Someone told his wife they had seen Jimmy performing in a booth bout and her husband did not deny it. There was an unholy row, but fortunately for Wilde his misconduct coincided with a pit strike. Now he was on short pay and there was a baby on the way. When there wasn't enough to pay the week's grocery bill, Jimmy murmured that he could always pick up a few bob at Scarrott's booth, and 'Lisbeth retorted that as he was a married man and would soon be a father, he had better do something about it.

James Wilde was out of the house before she had finished speaking, and became a regular booth fighter. On one occasion he took on 'all comers' for three-and-a-half hours, during which he scored nineteen knockouts. Then he rested for thirty minutes, won four more spectacular victories before the proprietor closed his establishment, and went home with the fantastic fortune of forty pounds in his pocket. He left the pits for good to make a career of glove-fighting, joining forces with a Cardiff sportsman, Teddy Lewis, who steered him to the top.

With Jimmy bringing in ten, then fifteen, then twenty pounds for a contest, 'Lizbeth's attitude towards boxing softened. She started to attend his bouts that were staged in the regular arenas; she trudged across the mountains with him to Caerphilly, carrying her four-month-old son, David, to watch her husband win a famous victory. She even sparred with him wearing a protector made from an old corset, to save the expense of employing another boxer, although such a precaution was hardly necessary, as Jimmy knew it would have been more than his life was worth to have hit her – even by accident.

His fame spread. Promoters in Liverpool, Glasgow, Leicester and Manchester sought his services. He made a brief visit to London's famous Ring in the Blackfriars Road, to score a sensational one-round knockout after the proprietor's wife, Mrs Dick Burge, had protested about letting a 'mere boy' get into the ring. Solemnly Jimmy assured her that he was a married man with a family, but she was still agitated until she sat open-mouthed as Wilde ducked, bobbed, feinted and threw the one punch that ended the fight.

Eventually the National Sporting Club sent for the tiny Welshman and off went an excited Jimmy to show his fistic wares in the famous Covent Garden establishment where he became a great favourite. His colourful style, his fearless attacking, his phenomenal punching, won him the admiration of all fight followers. The Prince of Wales, Lord Lonsdale, and other notable figures became his personal friends. The one-time begrimed little miner could now rub shoulders with the best in the land.

He was in his 23rd year before he knew what it was like to suffer defeat, but there were extenuating circumstances for this initial setback. Matched to fight James (Tancy) Lee from Glasgow in a twenty-round contest involving the British flyweight title and the Lonsdale Belt that went with it, Wilde contracted influenza a few days before the contest was due to take place, had a high temperature, and was in no condition to go into a ring. Manager Lewis wanted to ask for a postponement, but Wilde would not hear of it. This was his big chance after years of climbing the ladder. 'Lizbeth pleaded and threatened, but Jimmy was obstinate. Although feeling ill, he was sure he could make short work of his Scottish opponent and so come to no harm.

Although she knew that women were not permitted inside the National Sporting Club, Mrs Wilde accompanied her husband to London and stayed in a nearby hotel. There she waited for his triumphant return as flyweight champion of England. She was kept in suspense for a long time. Lee, a former amateur champion, was a tireless, durable and determined warrior who excelled at close-range fighting. Right from the start he bored into the stricken Welshman and pounded his frail body with a ceaseless two-fisted barrage. Wilde tried hard to keep him at bay, but his illness had taken the power out of his punches and as the rounds went by so his strength and stamina drained away.

By the seventeenth round he could barely stand, and after being floored several times, the towel came fluttering in from his corner. Teddy Lewis climbed through the ropes and picked up his battered boy. But when he realised that he had not been knocked out, Wilde was highly indignant. He considered that all the while he was conscious he should be allowed to go on fighting and made his manager promise that never again would he surrender on his behalf. It was an imposed vow that almost cost Jimmy his life in later years.

Lewis would have promised anything at that moment, for Wilde was in a sorry state. His lips were lacerated, his face a mass of bruises, his right ear swelling to an alarming degree. They got him to his dressing-room and worked over him, then it was decided that he must remain the night in the Club. That did it. He demanded that his wife be sent for and when he was reminded that this was impossible, it being a breach of the rules, he created such a scene, even threatening to throw himself out of the window. At last they gave in. Someone was sent to fetch 'Lizbeth from her hotel and, pulling a coat over her night-dress, she hurried to his side to become the first and only woman ever to stay over-night at the National Sporting Club.

Jimmy was out of the ring for two months, then went to work on the flys and bantams with increased destructiveness. Given a second chance to win the championship, he stopped Joe Symonds, from Plymouth, in twelve rounds, gained revenge over Lee in eleven rounds and won the Lonsdale Belt outright by beating George Clark in four rounds. He next defeated two imported Americans to gain recognition as world champion, then made a triumphant tour of the United States to return home after eleven bouts with nearly a hundred thousand dollars in purse money.

That was in 1920 and Jimmy was past 28. Behind him was

strewn a long trail of victims, to most of whom he had conceded considerable weight, even to flyweights, for he never scaled more than 104 pounds, and he had taken on big bantams, even featherweights. He could have retired at the height of his fame and glory, in fact, both he and 'Lizbeth agreed that the time had come for him to hang up his gloves for good. They bought a house at Radyr near Cardiff which they called 'Lonsdale'; there was money in the bank and a good sum in securities. And Mrs Wilde had her bag of diamonds.

She had come by these in an unusual way. During the 1914-18 War, Jimmy had served as a Sergeant-Instructor in the British Army. His duties kept him fit, and he was asked frequently to give boxing exhibitions to help entertain the troops. Several times he was given leave to take part in an actual contest when the proceeds were for a charitable cause. A party of sportsmen were anxious to promote an open-air show at Stamford Bridge in August 1918 and they wanted Wilde as their star attraction. As he had beaten every available fly and bantam, they proposed putting him in with Joe Conn, a London featherweight of high class.

A scientific instrument maker engaged on government work, Conn was free to accept a professional contest, but Wilde was a soldier. He could get leave to train for and take part in a public boxing match, but would not be allowed to accept any monetary payment. Jimmy would have been quite happy to box for nothing, but had the future to think about and defeat by Conn, five years younger and 21 pounds heavier, might ruin his reputation. He turned down the proposal, but the promoters were so keen to have his services that they offered to make him a present of any commodity he might choose in lieu of a cash payment.

He advised them to approach his wife and without any hesitation she plumped for diamonds, saying she did not possess any, but had always wanted some. How many she expected, I do not know, but the purse was three thousand pounds and she was delighted to receive a bagful after her talented husband had demolished his bigger opponent in the twelfth of their scheduled twenty-round bout. 'Lizbeth carried them around wherever she went until finally persuaded to put them in a bank for safe-keeping. So, with one thing and another, the Wildes seemed set to live a comfortable family life without it being necessary for Jimmy to go back into the ring.

Then out of the blue came an astounding offer of eight thousand pounds for him to fight at the Albert Hall against Pete Herman, the American holder of the world's bantam-weight championship. James looked at 'Lizbeth, 'Lizbeth looked at James. Eight thousand pounds was a fortune in those days; it was theirs for just one more fight. Although he had been out of action for over six month, Wilde had kept himself in fine physical trim. A nod from his wife and he told manager Teddy Lewis to go ahead and sign the contract. Then he pushed his training kit into a bag and went off to the gymnasium.

If ever a boxer was tricked out of winning a contest, Wilde was against Herman. In the first place he wanted the distance to be fifteen rounds, but had to agree to twenty because the promoters wanted to advertise the bout as for the world title and at that time all championship fights had to be fought over the marathon course. Then, very conveniently, Herman lost his bantam crown to fellow-countryman, Joe Lynch, a few days before leaving for England, so that Jimmy was inveigled into a full-length contest without the possibility of getting his rightful award in the event of victory. That the American regained his championship soon after returning home was regarded as proof of the duplicity.

There was also the vital question of weight. The bantam poundage was 118, which meant that Wilde would be conceding more than a stone. In the contract he stipulated there should be a ringside weigh-in, in order to reduce his disadvantage to the minimum, but when it came to the time for going into the ring, Herman flatly refused to go on the scales, knowing full well that he would be far above the contracted weight. When he heard this, Jimmy would not stir out of his dressing-room and a state of stalemate existed.

Eventually the capacity crowd got tired of looking at the empty ring and it began to get out of hand. There was hand-clapping, stamping, booing and whistling that got louder and more threatening as the minutes went by and there was still no sign of the principals in the feature contest of the evening. The Prince of Wales was in a ringside seat and when the roar of the crowd had become thunderous, he darted up the steps into the ring, held up his hand to produce instant silence, then made a short speech in which he requested them to be patient while the promoters tried to find a satisfactory solution to their problem.

The royal action had only temporarily calmed down the irate fans and there were still signs of an impending riot. When the news of what was going on in the arena was conveyed to Jimmy, he came to a quick decision: 'I don't want anyone to be embarrassed, let alone the Prince,' he said, getting up and making for the door of the dressing-room. 'Well, what are you waiting for?' he asked his astonished seconds, going out to face his doom.

Stronger, much heavier, and younger by four years, besides being a beautiful boxer, Herman gradually wore down Wilde. The gallant little Welshman fought back until he dropped; even then it was the referee who stopped the contest in the 17th round. 'I'm sorry about this, Jimmy,' he said, as he picked up the badly battered Wilde and took him to his corner. 'But you don't know the way to stay down and I'm not letting you take another punch.'

That should have been the end and, so far as 'Lizbeth was concerned, it was. But after he had been in retirement for two-and-a-half years, the Americans offered Wilde £13,000 to defend his world flyweight title against Pancho Villa, a young and vigorous Philippino. Teddy Lewis said No; Wilde's wife echoed him; Jimmy was keen. He still felt he was the best flyweight in the world and wanted to finish his fantastic career in a blaze of glory. Even when it was pointed out that he was a month past his 31st birthday, he still wanted to make the trip.

They argued for hours, two against one, until Mrs Wilde realised that if her husband was thwarted in this enterprise he would remember it for the rest of his life. She gave way for the simple reason that Jimmy wanted to do it. But she made sure that she went with him. It was a disastrous venture. Jimmy was ring-rusty, there was a heatwave in New York, and the championship fight took place in the Polo Grounds, attracting 23,000 fans eager to see if dynamic youth could triumph over age and experience.

Villa was a brown-skinned demon against a slow-footed veteran. He hit the Welshman almost at will, but Jimmy took his punishment bravely, walking through a deluge of punches to try and get in his own blows. He was dead weary when the bell sounded to end the sixth round and dropped his hands only to be struck on the point of the chin by a dazzling right that dropped him flat on his face. His seconds had to come in and carry him to his corner. Manager Lewis protested that the champion had been fouled, but the referee took the view that Villa's punch had been on its way when the timekeper signalled the end of the round.

There should never have been a seventh, but Wilde insisted on continuing. Only half-conscious of where he was or what was going on, he marched into the blazing fists of his determined opponent to go down like a true champion. 'Lizbeth at the ringside hid her face in her hands as they counted out her husband, then she followed his handlers as they took him to his corner, worked vainly over him and then had to carry him to the dressing-room. She sat by the rubbing-table while a doctor spent four hours in massaging him back to consciosness.

Wilde was removed to the home of some American friends where he made a slow recovery. It was three weeks before he recognised 'Lizbeth and the first thing he told her was that he would not fight any more. She looked at him tenderly and tears came into her eyes. She had already made up her mind about that, and now she intended to see that he kept his word.

14

Fame and Fortune Lost to Love

Randolph Turpin

Women can be as much a help as a hindrance to fighting men and Randolph Turpin, who suffered and benefited in turn from the women who came into his orbit during a fabulous boxing career, was no exception; in fact, there were too many in his short and bothered life. Born at Leamington Spa of a white mother and coloured father, he had to fight adversity from childhood, so that when he adopted fisticuffs as a profession, self-defence came automatically. His dad died from the effects of poison gas encountered in World War I when Randy, the youngest of five, was a mere nine months old.

With three boys and two girls to support, Mrs Turpin had to scrub floors to keep the home together. She also handed out some stern discipline and a good deal of common sense advice. Dick, the eldest, was boxing professionally in the Warwickshire booths almost from his schooldays. In this hard training ground, he learnt to become a master-boxer, and eventually a champion. His younger brothers, Jackie and Randy, worshipped him and could barely wait to become old enough to do some public scrapping themselves.

The Second World War started. Dick, who was already showing extreme promise as a middleweight, went off and served with the 8th Army from El Alamein to Berlin. Jackie went into the Merchant Navy, sisters Jean and Kathleen joined the W.A.A.F., but Randy had to wait until hostilities ended; then he went into the Royal Navy as a cook. Here he got plenty of opportunities to develop his boxing talent as an amateur, and won five titles, his crowning triumph being a one-round victory over Harold Anspach in a Great Britain *v.* America match at Wembley Pool.

Four months later the Leamington Larruper turned pro, and the destruction of the British middleweight division began. Randy went through his first eighteen contests in an aggregate of 55 rounds and when he beat the reigning champion, Vince Hawkins, only his youth prevented him from participating in a championship contest. Not that Mum would have let him take a title fight even if there were no age restrictions. 'Dick's the eldest and he is entitled to first chance,' she told the family. 'He's taught Randy all he knows, so that makes him the best in my reckoning.'

She also damped any ideas that the brothers should box one another in serious combat. 'They can fight as fierce as they like in the gym, but one won't strike the other in public all the time I'm alive.' So Dick fought for the championship and beat Hawkins on points to become the first coloured boxer to win a British title.

Subsequently he lost the crown to Albert Finch, but Randy restored the family honour by winning back the title with a spectacular five-round conquest. But a lot had happened in the meantime. At 18 Randy had met and married Mary Theresa Stack, an Irish girl working in a Warwick hotel whose brother Michael was also a professional boxer.

Unfortunately it started to go wrong within a few months, and in little more than a year they had separated and she had brought an action against him for assault. Randy denied the charges and eventually the case was dismissed, but it was a worrying time for a youngster embarking on a hazardous boxing career.

Just before he entered the ring to fight Jean Stock, the French middleweight champion, Turpin was informed that his baby son had been given into the legal custody of his wife. It was a shattering blow and he told brother Dick as he sat in the dressing-room: 'If I get licked, don't be surprised. I never felt less like fighting than I do tonight.' He was licked all right. Showing nothing like his true, devastating form, Randy crumpled before the masterly fists of the tough Frenchman and at the end of five punishing rounds he told his handlers he could not go on.

The result was a distinct shock to all those who fancied they saw Randy as a future world-beater. In fact, some of the sceptics forecast that the ring had seen the last of the young Leamington lad. So it had – for five months, then back he came with a tremendous run of thirteen brilliant victories that were rounded off by his defeat of Finch for the British middleweight crown at the age of 22.

There was no stopping Turpin now, and Promoter Jack Solomons gave him every opportunity to gain more success in London while Midland promoters eagerly sought his services and were rewarded with big audiences and thrilling performances as the Licker pounded his rivals. He took the European title with a 48-second win over Dutchman Luc van Dam; he gained revenge over Stock by stopping him in five rounds, and went on unbeaten until the night he brought off the unbelievable and outpointed Sugar Ray Robinson to become middleweight champion of the world in 1951.

Some people criticised Solomons for making the match, arguing that Turpin was far too young to take on a man of Robinson's high calibre. But Randy treated it as just another contest, and thrilled the 18,000 fans who packed out the Exhibition Hall at Earl's Court with a confident box-fighting display that saw him returned the winner of a close contest. Randy was Britain's hero of the hour, and no boxer in ring history has ever enjoyed so much publicity and popularity. In London they jammed the streets to see him, in his home-town they gave him a civic reception. For the first time he received a staggering fan mail, mostly from women admirers. Those that wrote came from all classes and were of all ages from schoolgirls to matrons; some became nuisances and Randy was glad that he was obliged to give Robinson a return title fight in America within three months. Even when this was reduced to 64 days to suit the New York promoters he raised no objection – it was a welcome respite to get away from it all.

In the Catskill Mountains, a hundred miles out of New York, Turpin settled down to prepare for the second encounter with Sugar Ray. He had his manager, trainer and brothers Dick and Jackie with him and there was every confidence that he would keep his title. The fight was the talk of America and over 61,000 fans packed into the Polo Grounds to create an attendance record for any fight below heavyweight. They got full value for their money.

In the early rounds Robinson dominated the exchanges, clearly determined to win back his lost crown. But Turpin kept pace with him and from the half-way stage began to make up any lee-way and forge ahead. There was concern in the American's corner when it was realised that Randy seemed as strong as when he started, whereas Sugar Ray was feeling the pace. There was consternation when Robinson sustained an ugly wound over his left eye during a gruelling scrimmage in the ninth.

They patched it up, but a right from Randy ripped it open at the start of the next round, and now the Turpin fans were cheering him on and it looked as though he might go one better this time and stop the American. Things were serious for Robinson and no one knew it more than Sugar Ray. He was being backed round the ring with Turpin pitching leather at him from both hands. Blood was streaming down his left cheek, the referee was watching the wound; there was the distinct possibility that he would not allow the American to come out for the eleventh round.

Something desperate had to be done and Sugar Ray did it. From long range he tossed over a right that he fondly hoped would prove the pay-off. It was one that Randy should have blocked or dodged, instead he took it full force on the point of his chin. Down he went to lay strewn like a giant starfish and although he beat the count he had been badly shocked. Into the ropes he went and then, with the killer instinct surging into his brain, Robinson smashed at him unmercifully in an effort to put him down for good. But he could not do it. Turpin took it all and might have lasted out the round, but the referee decided he had taken enough. With only a few seconds remaining, the fight was stopped and Randy was an ex-world champ.

After the fight some of Randy's training camp visitors threw a party in Harlem and this was just what a disappointed fighter needed. There he met Adele Daniels, a coloured girl, and they became very friendly. At that moment he was awaiting his divorce from Mary and was in the right mood for feminine company. The friendship grew and Adele came to the docks to see him off to England. There was talk of a third fight with Robinson and no doubt they did not expect to be separated for long; she alleged afterwards that he promised to marry her as soon as his wife had secured her divorce.

The chance to win back the world middleweight title did not mature. Instead Randy beat Don Cockell for the light-heavyweight championship and spent the next two years in licking all comers, including Charles Humez, of France, in a contest labelled as for the world middleweight crown, Sugar Ray having decided to retire. This victory meant that Turpin would now face the American champion, Carl (Bobo) Olson of Hawaii, for the undisputed title. No man had brighter prospects and Randy made his second trip to the States with everyone anticipating he would return as world champion once again.

Turpin should have gone off light-hearted and confident, yet his frame of mind was completely in the reverse. His divorce had been granted, but now he had met and fallen in love with Gwenneth Price, a Welsh girl; it was agreed that on his return, winner or loser, they would get married. It is the greatest pity that she did not accompany him to New York, for no sooner had he reached his hotel than Miss Daniels turned up eager to renew their association. Randy had to tell her that things were different now, that he planned to get married on his return home. His frankness was his undoing and if he had never heard of what happens to a woman scorned, he knew it now.

Adele made a scene and many scenes and Randy went to his training camp in a very worried state of mind. His heart was in Wales and his troubles were in New York. He was in no mood to prepare for the most vital fight of his career and although it came as a great shock to his thousands of supporters in this country when he was soundly beaten by Olson, the result was not surprising to those who knew the true state of affairs. In addition to having Mary, Adele and Gwenneth on his mind, he was being cited as co-respondent in a divorce suit being brought by a Lancashire policeman against his wife for alleged adultery with Turpin when he was training at Gwych Castle in North Wales. It was an ugly situation that had to be faced as soon as he got back to England.

Before he could leave New York he was arrested and taken into court with his name smeared in the newspaper headlines. Once she realised that she had no future with Randy, Adele let him have the full force of her fury, charging him with assault and rape and sueing him for a hundred thousand dollars. In the end she accepted a fraction of this sum, but this and the legal costs made a big hole in Turpin's American earnings and he returned home sadder and wiser to marry Gwenneth and find eventual happiness.

The boxing career continued for five more years with some more great wins and some sad setbacks. Twice more he became British light-heavyweight champion to win a Lonsdale Belt outright, but announced his retirement after losing inside two rounds to Yolande Pompey at Birmingham in 1958.

When he finally hung up the gloves he could look back with pride on a truly great record, but now he was assailed by new troubles in the form of income tax demands running into thousands of pounds. For some reason he had not met the demands as he received them; now he was faced with a massive debt. He obtained work in a scrap metal yard, he earned money at all-in wrestling, he took over a transport cafe and served in the kitchen. By now he had four daughters to feed and clothe and still he was being harrassed by Inland Revenue officers. One morning in 1966 he went into the attic bedroom, fired two shots at his youngest child, then turned the revolver fatally on himself. In a career lasting twelve years and 71 bouts, he had earned an estimated £300,000 with his fists. Yet he died practically penniless, a lot of his money having been squandered on his amatory adventures.

15

Mae's Blind Faith Brought Disaster

Tommy Collins

If you happen to be born into a family of sixteen and come of poor parents domiciled in the tenement district of Boston known as South End, fighting becomes a sheer necessity, especially if you are a skinny, undersized kid like Tommy Collins. To add to his life handicaps, he was born in 1929 at a time when the biggest industrial slump America had ever known was at its peak; as a tender child he was roaming the streets, ragged and barefooted, looking for scraps.

Collins' father was an Irish labourer who never missed an opportunity for fistic indulgence. Tommy inherited this trait and was rarely short of someone to scrap with. He fought his brothers and sisters for the right to live; the boy upstairs and the boy downstairs for the honour of the tenement building; the street corner kids to justify his existence, and the boys at school for the sheer love of it.

He was pale and thin, but from somewhere he had acquired the art of hitting with tremendous power. His bony fists on the end of pipe-stem arms would lash out with amazing force and perfect timing. Soon he was knocking kids out and, of course, that provoked plenty of parental protest. In the end someone told John Conlon, a guard at the local jail, and he took Tommy along to an amateur boxing club and turned him loose.

The instructor there made one attempt to teach the South End boy something of the Art of Boxing and then gave it up. Collins' personal brand of belligerency was to wade in two-fistedly and fight like fury until the opposition caved in. Any attempt to change that was a sheer waste of time. Tommy won the New England flyweight championship when he was sixteen and qualified for the national title in the Boston Garden, but broke his thumb in the final and lost on points.

As soon as the fracture had healed, the boy urged his mentor to let him turn professional. He had been working for a year on an ice delivery truck, but most of his wages went into the family fund. Now he wanted to augment his earnings in the paid ring. The Boston Garden was run by Sam Silverman and his partner, Rip Valenti, a tavern proprietor. The latter took a half-interest in Collins, John Conlon became co-manager, and they proceeded to exploit the local lad in a maximum capacity.

In the first three years Tommy had forty bouts of which he won 35, ending 24 of them inside the scheduled distance. By that time he had become the talk of the town and the fans flocked to see this cocky, bright-eyed kid go breezing into action with both fists blazing and not a glove raised in self-defence. Of the five contests he lost, three were stopped. Not because Collins was being badly punished, but because he was suffering such severe facial cuts that the referee thought he might bleed to death.

Only man to knock him out was a lanky coloured featherweight named Spider Armstrong, who survived two early knockdowns and belted Tommy into the canvas when he ran out of gas in the fifth round. Tommy was sitting dejectedly in the dressing-room having his usual emergency-ward treatment, when someone tapped on the door and they told him there was a girl outside who claimed she was a nurse.

'If she's pretty, let her in,' ordered Tommy and his dream girl walked in. She was beautiful Mae McAllister, employed at the Boston City Hospital, and she blushingly confessed that she was a staunch Collins fan. 'You see you stop that way,' grinned Tommy through his lacerations and bruises. And to make sure, he married her soon afterwards and she immediately took a big interest in his fistic welfare.

With her unstinted admiration and encouragement, her husband became even more cocky and brash than he had been in his bachelor days. Tony Canzoneri, a great champion of yesteryear, was visiting the Boston gymnasium when Collins was working out. Tommy was bounding round the big bag and making a lot of noise and the man who had beaten the best feathers and lightweights in his historic career, asked who he was.

'I'm Tommy Collins, the next featherweight champion,' said the youngster coming over to the group. 'It's a good thing I wasn't around when you were boxing.' Canzoneri looked the kid up and down then quietly said that he was right, adding that had they met he would in all probability have been charged with murder. Then he walked out and the unabashed Tommy went back to his bag.

Collins would not rest until his managers arranged a return match with Armstrong, then he told all and sundry that he would win this one by a knockout. He was so emphatic that the word went round that the fight was fixed and the Boxing Commission sent for Tommy and warned him what to expect if there was any funny business. If it was found that Tommy's opponent had agreed to lay down, Collins would lose his licence and be banned from boxing in every State. 'Of course, it's fixed,' snorted the local firebrand. 'He's going out in the second round, but *he* doesn't know it.' And that's just how it ended.

In 1951, when he was just 22, Tommy won the New England featherweight title in sensational fashion, knocking out Joey Cam in the first round. It was a win that rocketed him to his highest peak in fistic stardom; it was a victory that turned the heads of all his associates. Mae, who had been sitting ringside and rooting vigorously during the short-lived championship fight, held up her cheek for a kiss as her triumphant husband came down the aisle on his way back to the dressing-room.

She followed him and wasn't at all surprised when Tommy told the newspaper men that he was now after Sandy Saddler for the world title. At that time they both thought Tommy was invicible. His co-managers blenched at the thought. Saddler was a truly great champion. He had been around a long time and was at his peak. Still the Boston fans clamoured for the fight and Sandy agreed to take Collins for ten rounds, with the promise of a title scrap if he should win.

Tommy had the crowd roaring madly in the first round when he stormed into the lathy champion and sent him rolling in the resin with a zooming right to the chin. Only the compulsory eight-seconds count saved Saddler from being knocked out and when the contest was resumed Collins went punch crazy.

His furious non-stop attack had Saddler bewildered; he was fighting for his very life. Tommy was tossing punches from his shoe tops and from the small of his back, in the third he split Sandy's left eyebrow into a scarlet gash. The fans were wild with excitement and when they saw the bruised and battered champion go to the wrong corner at the end of the fourth round, they raised the roof.

By the fifth, however, Collins began to blow up. He paused to take a breather and was promptly nailed by a sizzling left hook to the ribs that shook him down to his toes. Like lightning, Sandy banged a left hook on the Boston boy's chin and down he went, all the fight knocked out of him. Even so, Saddler had to floor him three more times before the referee decided that all hope of a Collins victory had gone.

That might have been a lesson, but three months later Tommy took on Willie Pep, who had lost the 9st. title to Saddler. The former champ was on the comeback trail, he thought a Boston win would boost his stock. 'Listen, Tommy,' said the ring-wise Pep after the weigh-in. 'You be a good boy out there tonight. Don't get fresh and I'll box you around a bit and make you look good before your own folk. But don't get wise, see.' 'Willie,' laughed Collins. 'Don't be silly. I'm going to knock you out tonight. That's something you can bank on.'

In the sixth round he had Pep standing on one ear after four knockdowns and the bout was stopped. After that Tommy beat Ronnie Clayton, the British titleholder, in five rounds; Lauro Salas, former world lightweight champion, on points, and punched the stuffing out of Fabela Chavex – all Boston bouts that had the fans raving.

Mrs Collins was so proud of her husband that she suggested that he should challenge for the featherweight championship of the world. She coaxed him into thinking that he had all but beaten Saddler and deserved a second chance, but this time the title would have to be at stake. But Tommy's managers could not get the coloured champion to risk his crown against the Boston Terror. Sandy had been called up for the United States Army, so they had to look around for another star opponent.

They couldn't have aimed higher than Jimmy Carter, who had won, lost and regained the world lightweight championship during the past two years. He was six years older and half a stone heavier than Collins, had been actively engaged in the profession for seven years and fought the best in the business. His record was studded with wins inside the distance.

Yes, the coloured lightweight king would defend his title against the Bostonian in Boston, which was a distinct sign of confidence seeing that the Bean City was noted for its home-town decisions. Everyone was ready for a gala occasion, the crowning of the local hero. Mae even went to the Massachussetts Boxing Commission and applied for a licence as her husband's trainer and second. What is more, she got it. They had just had their first baby and before leaving for the arena Tommy promised his wife that she would be home in time to feed it. He kept his word.

When they climbed into the ring, the 12,500 fans stood up and cheered Tommy as if he had been the President. They made so much noise that Carter's entry was barely noticed and he did not get as much as a cheer when announced. Tommy, clad in green trunks, green socks with green boot-laces, danced round the champion in the first round, made a few charges and Carter was content to let him burn up some energy.

In the second round Collins darted from his corner, gave his little war cry and set about the lightweight king with great gusto. Carter met the onslaught with a barrage of two-fisted body punches, the like of which his young opponent had never before experienced.

Tommy took the first shock of these with customary gameness and bounded in for more. He got them with added venom and when Jimmy switched to the head, Tommy's boxing brain was quickly paralysed. What fighting he did now was completely innocuous and did not for a moment deter the champion in his merciless course of destruction. Collins zig-zagged his way back to his corner. They hastily restored him to some semblance of fitness and sent him out again.

The first blow from Carter, a vicious right hook, sent the Boston boy slithering to the canvas. He got up and was promptly knocked off his feet again. Each time the champion struck, his picked punch sent Tommy staggering and had him cutting crude gestures as he floundered off balance and hit the floor with a crash.

Seven times he was put down for counts and seven times he got up. In that fearful three minutes, the longest Mae had ever known, the referee made no move to stop the massacre. He even allowed the cruelly battered local boy to come out for the fourth. As soon as he got into range, Carter floored him again, and now the fans were screaming for the slaughter to be stopped. But Tommy had to take two further counts before the referee was satisfied that he had had enough. Ten knockdowns in seven minutes and 28 seconds. What were they seeking – a boxing record?

That should have convinced anyone that Collins had got as far as he would ever get in the Fight Game. From the Carter fight he had collected 38,000 dollars. In his last dozen contests he had earned a considerable fortune, most of which Mae had carefully salted away. There was no reason for him to fight again, but Tommy wasn't convinced that he was through. It took a red-headed coloured boy named Teddy Davis to do that in a ten-round beating that told the avid Boston fans that they must start looking for another local hero. Tommy Collins – at 24 – never fought again.

16

Katie Took
Him to the Heights

Lew Jenkins

It was a busy morning at Stillman's famous gymnasium on
54th Street and 8th Avenue, in New York. The fight mob was
filling the place out, the air was thick with punches and smoke.
Up the stairs came a thin, lantern-jawed lightweight, and on
his arm was a small but beautiful red-head, who looked as if
she had just stepped out of a film magazine.

The man at the turnstile shook his head. 'You, yes,' he said,
'but, the dame, no.' 'I'm Lew Jenkins and she's my wife,'
answered the boxer in a noticeable Texan drawl. 'And I am his
trainer and second and have a licence,' she added. They were
informed that it made no difference – women were barred from
watching the fighters work out.

Lou Stillman strolled over and sized up the situation. He
noticed that Mrs Jenkins was wearing a sports jacket and
slacks, and instructed the doorman to let them both in on the
payment of ten cents each. That was the Jenkins' entry into
big-time boxing, inspired and manoeuvred by Katie, who had
the utmost belief in the power behind her husband's bony
right hand.

They had been married a year now and had come from
Dallas via Chicago. Katie was twenty – a hundred pounds'
worth of bubbling energy with plenty of adventure in her heart.
A skilled stock-car driver, she turned over three times one
afternoon, crawled out of the wreck and limped off the track
into the arms of a grinning onlooker. He dusted her down, said
that he admired her courage and asked if she would like a cup
of coffee. While they were drinking it he told her his name was
Lew Jenkins and that he was boxing in the carnival adjoining

the race track. He had just won a fight and was taking time out before going back for another. 'I'm Katie Jenkins,' she replied. 'And I am not doing so bad, neither'.

The similarity in their names made them both laugh and then wonder if there was any future in the coincidence. Looking into the biggest and most beautiful eyes he had ever seen, Lew suggested that there were one too many Jenkins in the world and Katie agreed. She suggested they might team up to their mutual advantage. But not in Texas. Fighters made money in the big cities and if they were going to seek fame and fortune it would mean travelling East. Surveying his lean, craggy face with the pale blue eyes that carried a hint of the 'killer' behind them, Katie knew that he could make more money throwing punches than she could at motor racing and three weeks later they were married.

She took off her wristwatch and pawned it for sixty dollars. Lew took the money and bought a very second-hand car. Into it they piled their few possessions and the trail for fistic fortune began. There were 27 contests in 1938, but most of them ended so quickly in Lew's favour that they hardly counted. There were a few defeats, mainly because he got cut up before he could land his leveller, but Katie got herself into his corner whenever the State laws allowed, to patch him up and give him the utmost in encouragement. In addition, she parleyed with promoters, shook off the sharks and conducted her husband's business with firm intent. And when they neared the big-time, she had enough sense to engage a manager of repute to take over while she concentrated on securing the right sort of publicity.

Lew had spent some years in the United States Cavalry and was at home on a horse. In New York she had him rigged out as a cowboy and sent him galloping around Central Park. She attended him in the gymnasium with workmanlike efficiency; she put on the charm when they attended functions. They became a colourful pair who were constantly in the sporting pages. It was a new twist in the Fight Game and the scribes fell for it.

There were four winning fights in a small arena on Long

Island, then they moved into the city itself and Lew started a series of knockout wins that were to take him to the top. The fans sat up and stared when Primo Flores was stopped in five rounds and when Mike Belloise, former featherweight champion, was finished in seven.

They packed into Madison Square Garden when Mike Jacobs matched the smart Canadian champion, Billy Marquart, with Texan Lew, most of them expecting Katie's husband to get a real hiding. Mrs Jenkins was not allowed to exercise her second's licence in New York, but she sat close by Lew's corner and gave him vocal support in a ladylike manner.

For two rounds, and well into the third, Marquart battered the Texan. He drove Jenkins back into the ropes and tried his utmost to finish him. The fans were yelling for the 'kill'. Katie screamed at Lew to do something, but he had his back to her. He must have heard her above the din, it was shrill enough, for suddenly he laid back and belted his right at Billy's chin.

It landed flush and the Canadian was sent staggering back across the ring. Lew leapt upon him, punched him viciously into the ropes with both hands, then hammered him down, smashing away even when Marquart was on the canvas, halfway out of the ring. The referee hauled the berserk boxer off; Lew struggled free and clouted the stricken Canadian again. This time the referee marched Jenkins off to a neutral corner; Marquart when he returned to him was a mere heap on the floor whom the timekeeper had counted out.

Overnight Jenkins was a ring hero, the most vicious fighter and the most savage puncher at his weight they had seen in years. Everyone wanted to fête the Jenkinses, but although Lew was willing enough, Katie shook her glossy head and said that they were going back to Texas for Christmas. As the promoter in Dallas had given Jenkins his first opportunities, they would give him a fight, see their respective families and be back in the New Year.

All Dallas turned out to greet them. They were offered free residence at the best hotel, but Katie chose the one they had always used in the old days. They attended civic receptions and were given a wonderful time. They had their first quarrel. At 2 a.m. one morning Katie nudged Lew's elbow: 'It's your bed-time, honey. Tomorrow you start training again, remember?' Her husband complained that the party was not yet over and was informed that it had ended so far as he was concerned. 'You pay me three dollars a day to train you and I want to start earning again,' she snapped.

Very reluctantly Lew followed her home, but from then onwards she found it harder to keep his nose to the grindstone. 'You'll get all the time in the world to be a playboy,' she counselled, 'but for now let's concentrate on making you the lightweight champion of the world.' Jenkins won his Dallas contest in a round, then the call came for another Garden fight, this time with leading contender, Tippy Larkin, in what would be regarded as a final eliminator for the title.

New York welcomed them royally again, but the critics did not give the Texan much of a chance. Larkin was a smart boxer with a fine record. He would cut Lew to ribbons while making him miss with his haymakers. Katie had to keep close watch on her husband to get him fighting fit. Nursing a grievance against her when he went into the ring he took it out of Larkin.

Tippy skipped round Lew at a fast gait for the first two minutes without taking a punch. He had the Texan's nose bleeding from stinging lefts while he easily dodged his rival's big rights. Suddenly Jenkins threw one a shade faster and aimed at a point into which he reckoned Larkin would move. Tippy took the blow full on the chin and went out like a light. Time: 2 min. 41 sec. of the opening round.

That night promoter Jacobs told Katie that her husband would be fighting Lou Ambers for the lightweight title in two months' time. 'Get him here in shape and you'll be married to a champion,' Uncle Mike told her. He gave Katie a hard look; he had heard all about Lew's hankerings for the bright lights and tinsel. 'He'll be fit to fight for his life,' she promised.

Over 13,000 fans packed into the Garden to see how Ambers would deal with the Texan One-Punch. Lou had been around for nine years as a pro, with a hundred paid amateur fights before that. He had held the lightweight title for four years, losing it to Henry Armstrong and winning it back again. The bookies made him a 3 to 1 favourite. 'Go in and make me proud of you,' Katie urged her husband as he climbed into the ring. Under her strict supervision he had got into the finest condition of his life.

They fenced for thirty seconds, then Lew whipped over his right. It hit the champion full in the face and knocked him clean off his feet. Ambers scrambled to one knee, looked for his corner, nodded, and rose at 'five'. He then went into fast reverse with Jenkins following hot foot, his right hand cocked for another knockdown delivery.

In the second Ambers stabbed and uppercut his attacking rival at will and it looked as though he had fully recovered from the first round shock and would now set about the challenger and put him in his place. But just before the bell Lew struck again, a vicious right that bowled over the champion for the second time. Again he took 'five' and was then rushed into the ropes and hammered severely. The bell sounded, but Lew did not hear. Ambers dropped his hands and had to take two savage clouts on the chin before the referee and Jenkins' handlers could haul him off.

Ambers was a beaten man after that. His seconds worked hard over him, but he could offer little resistance when he came wavering up for round three. The fans were shrieking at the Texan to make a job of it; Katie was praying silently. Lew strode forth and with his first punch knocked the champion silly, then flattened him with the next. Lou took seven seconds this time, then was rushed into and through the ropes under a savage onslaught. The champ was hanging over the middle strand and Jenkins leaned over the top one to take another shot at him. The referee pulled Lew away and Ambers managed to get back into the ring, but was quickly felled by lefts and rights to the head. Now the fans were yelling for the fight to be stopped, but the referee let it go on. It was enough for Ambers' manager, however. He tossed in a towel, climbed into the ring and picked up his beaten boy.

There was no holding Lew now. Katie kept pace with him for a bit, then let him have his head. She knew he would be back when his money was spent or another fight was due. She liked the idea when Promoter Jacobs suggested the fight of the year – a match at 10st. between her husband and the reigning welterweight king, the mighty Henry Armstrong. Both knew it would be a money-spinner, too big for the Garden. It would mean the biggest purse of Jenkins' career – a small fortune and no risk of losing his title.

Lew liked the idea too. But in the intervening two months he barely went near a punch-bag. He spent money like water and did the wildest things, such as tearing up Broadway on a 90 m.p.h. motor cycle, hiring and abandoning fast cars all over the place, causing riots in restaurants. Sometimes he was missing for several days, but eventually Katie delivered him to the New York Polo Grounds on time and then had the mortification of seeing her out-of-condition husband take the hiding of his young life.

For three rounds he hammered Armstrong with everything he had got, but the famous triple-champion let him exhaust his limited stamina and then gave him such a two-fisted pounding about the body that Lew collapsed and by round six the fight had to be stopped to save him from being killed.

The Jenkinses bought a fine house at Palm Island, Miami, but the boxing partnership and the marriage was on the break-up. Lew resented his wife's continued interest in his boxing career and the way she tried to keep him on the straight-and-narrow between fights. They parted, and in little more than a year he had become an ex-champion, losing his title to Sammy Angott, and then, soon after that, a washed-up fighter. He parted from Katie and joined the U.S. Navy; on the Normandy beaches he heard that she had obtained a divorce. After that, so far as big-time boxing was concerned, Texas Lew had become just a memory.

17

His Mother Taught Him to Fight

Bold Bendigo

Most mothers are averse to their sons taking up a boxing career, but not buxom Mrs Thompson of Nottingham. Herself a great follower of the Prize Ring, she encouraged her son William from infancy, inspiring him with the glowing stories of the great champions of England who had fought with bare knuckles to achieve lasting fame. She also taught him the rudiments of the Noble Art, showing him the moves and the punches and clouting him on the ear with the flat of her broad hand if he made an error. The tuition was tough but complete, it being well known that she could hold her own with almost any man in the county when it came to settling an argument with the fists.

Of the 21 children she brought into the world, he was her favourite. One of triplets, she would have named him Abednego, after one of the biblical trio (Shadrach, Meshach and Abednego), but her husband would not hear of it. He insisted it should be plain William, and having laid down the law, he laid down again and died, leaving her to do as she pleased. William was the last of her large brood and at 21, when he announced his intention of trying his fortunes at fisticuffs, she was the proudest woman in the land.

Strongly built, well-muscled and standing 5ft 9½in., he stood before her as a splendid specimen of manhood. All his young life had been devoted to sport, and he excelled in all its branches, especially at acrobatics, wrestling and boxing. With twinkling eyes to match his dancing feet, young Will had a witty tongue, a cheerful grin and an easy manner that made him popular with everyone but his opponents. He was always ready to make a fool of himself for the sake of a laugh, and could have been just as successful as a circus clown as he was to prove as a boxer.

'There's Jem Burns' boxing booth at the fair, today,' he told his mother. 'And I'm going there to see if I can win the five pounds he's offering for anyone who can stand up to his lad from Newcastle. If I win, I'll ask him to take me into his troupe.' 'You'll do well, son,' she replied. 'I have it in my bones that I've brought a future champion of England into the world and it's you who will one day wear the belt that Jem Ward proudly owns. You have a mother's blessing son, and with it a mascot that will bring you luck.'

She rummaged in a dresser drawer and brought out a faded blue neckerchief covered with white spots. 'It's the famous Blue Birdseye, William, worn by one of Bristol's great fighters,' and there was a moistness in her eyes as she tied it round his neck. She warned him not to give it to his sweetheart and when he told her he hadn't got one, she grimly replied that if she caught any wench wearing it, she would spoil her looks for her. Will kissed his mother and strutted off, light of limb and heart, eager to get to the boxing booth and make his challenge. He knew that he just had to win, for he dare not go home if he lost.

The booth owner looked at the young man's eager face and thought his money was safe, but in the third round the Newcastle lad was knocked helpless on the canvas and the fight was stopped. Young Thompson joined the booth and was an instant success. Apart from his speed, agility and sharp hitting, he had a style that completely befoxed his opponents, standing right foot foremost, one of the first 'southpaws' the ring had ever seen. At first he used the name Abednego, just to please his mother, but when a fight of his was written up in the sporting papers, it became Bendigo and there it stuck. It is interesting to note that a famous racehorse was to bear the name he made so illustrious, while a town in Australia, north-west of Melbourne, has been called after him.

At nearby Hucknall there was Big Ben Caunt, looked upon by his supporters as likely to be the next champion. He stood

6ft 2½in., and weighed 15st.: a bear of a man with mighty strength and powerful punching. When Bendigo announced that he fancied himself to beat the giant, his friends thought he had gone mad. It meant giving away three stones and five inches in height, too big a handicap, they thought, against a man of Caunt's reputation.

Few accompanied Bendy when he walked over to Hucknall to have a try-out with the local favourite. Big Ben's supporters wagered 4 to 1 that he would stop the Nottingham youth in ten minutes, but at the end of that time Bendigo was still on his feet and unmarked, whereas Caunt left the ring with a split cheek. As a result the pair were matched in a fight to a finish for £25-a-side and Bendy had no difficulty in raising the money.

His supporters turned out in full force this time. They called themselves the 'Nottingham Lambs', but there was nothing lamb-like about them; they gave forth a mighty lion's roar when he scored 'first blood' with a neat jab to the nose. Caunt raised his hand to wipe away the gore, but Bendy did it for him with another smart left. Big Ben swung and missed, while his rival struck him at will. And whenever the giant went into grab the smaller man and toss him to the turf, Bendy slipped through his fingers and sat down of his own accord, grinning all over his face.

Caunt's followers kept calling for a 'foul', arguing that Bendigo was going down without taking a punch. But the umpires ruled that the Nottingham man had merely slipped. This seemed to happen whenever Bendy was in danger and by the end of the 22nd round Caunt's patience was exhausted. He rushed over to the opposite corner where Bendy was sitting on his second's knee. 'Will you stand up and fight fair, you tricky hound?' roared Big Ben. But all he got in return was an innocent smile. It was too much. Caunt let fly with a terrific back-hander that caught Bendigo on the chin and knocked him sprawling in the grass. The 'Lambs' screamed for a 'foul' and the umpires decided that as Caunt had struck the blow before the call of 'time', he had earned disqualification.

It was a great day for Bendigo. His manner of winning had

been unsatisfactory, but he'd won and was the hero of Nottingham. He rode back on the top of a coach, surrounded by the rip-roaring 'Lambs', on the way passing his mother who had trudged to Hucknall and stood on the fringe of the crowd as he fought Ben Caunt. Bendy waved his Blue Birdseye colours and Mrs Thompson waved back with a scarf of the same hue.

When they reached the nearest inn the party went in to celebrate, and Bendy soon heard someone enquiring after him. It was John Gully, former Champion of England, and now mine owner, racehorse owner and Member of Parliament. 'I like your style,' he told the astonished Bendigo. 'With the right tuition you could win the champion's belt. I suggest you go to Liverpool and put yourself under Jem Ward. If you go, I'll back you against the best in the country.' It was a wonderful offer and Bendigo did not hesitate. Ward was undefeated as Champion of England and the Belt hung in his Merseyside tavern. He welcomed Bendigo and found he had the right material to work with.

Bendy's mother had urged his departure, but a little gipsy fortune-teller with whom he had become acquainted was not so happy. She wanted him to stick to the booths where they could continue to see each other. 'The cards say that you must choose between true love and great fame,' she told him, but it was a waste of time. Bendy put winning the championship before anything else. He gave her a swift kiss and got on the stage coach for Liverpool. There was anger in her dark eyes as she watched him go.

Under the old champion he made enormous strides, beating Young Brassey, from Bradford, in 52 rounds; Charley Langan, from Dublin, in 32 rounds and Bill Looney in 99 rounds, all stubborn, gruelling contests in which Bendigo always finished up the fresher. The championship was now claimed for Bendigo, and Ward and Gully took him to London to meet the Fancy – the cream of sporting aristocrats who patronised the Prize Ring. Here he found many more friends and backers, and here he met his former gipsy sweetheart, who had become a Haymarket barmaid and was even more beautiful in his eyes.

She knew all about his successes, but had her heart set on marrying a lord. To stall Bendigo off she told him to first get the championship belt from Jem Ward and then ask her to marry him.

Ben Caunt came on the scene again. He had backing for a £100 contest against Bendigo and a return match was made to take place at Selby in Yorkshire. Once again Bendy proved too artful and skilful for his bigger opponent and soon poor Ben was bruised and bleeding. Bendigo was handicapped, however, by having to box in a pair of ordinary shoes, his own spiked ones having miraculously disappeared just before his entry into the ring.

This made him less nimble than usual and in the 13th round Caunt seized him round the waist. But instead of throwing the smaller man to the ground, Big Ben lifted him off his feet and held him in a bear-like hug, squeezing every drop of breath from his body. Bendy's face went purple and he was in danger of being suffocated. The Nottingham Lambs howled at Caunt to fight fair, but Ben only squeezed the harder, finally bending his rival across the ropes as if he intended to break his back.

Someone hacked through the hemp, both fighters pitched to the turf and the round was declared ended. When they came up again Bendigo skipped round the ring to escape Caunt's grasping arms, going down as soon as Big Ben got near him. Now it was the other side that was shouting for a 'foul' and in the 75th round the referee suddenly left the ring announcing that Bendigo had been disqualified.

There was an uproar from his followers, especially as the half-blinded Caunt seemed on the point of collapsing. Quick as a flash, Bendy snatched the colours from the ring post and made off. By rights they belonged to Big Ben and there was a hue and cry after Bendigo, but he made a safe getaway. Next day he sent them to his sweetheart in London for safe-keeping, but she had heard of his defeat and double-crossed him by handing them over to Caunt's supporters, thus establishing Bendy's downfall. For the first time after a fight he daren't face his mother.

The saddened Bendy saw a chance to regain favour by

challenging James (Deaf) Burke. They met in the small village of Heather in Leicestershire and, strange to relate, Bendigo won yet another battle on the disqualification of his rival. He won a moral victory before a blow was struck by insisting that Burke should remove a truss he was wearing. When Burke pleaded that he was ruptured and could not fight without it, Bendigo replied that *he* did not need one, so off it must come. What with this ruction and the Nottingham lad's tantalising tactics, the Deaf 'Un lost his temper in the tenth, butted his tormentor in the face and was promptly ruled out.

Bendy could go home. His mother made a great fuss and told him that while he was fighting Burke she had been sitting by the fire listening to the clock ticking. 'It kept saying: "Ben-dy, Ben-dy",' she said and added: 'If it had said "Burke", I'd have bashed its silly face in.'

Bendigo's backers wanted a third fight with Caunt to settle the question of superiority and it came off at Stony Stratford before ten thousand excited spectators. It was almost a repetition of their previous battles. Bendigo was like a jumping-jack, dancing round the giant and landing telling punches to the face. Hardly a round went by without one or the other claiming a foul and in the 93rd round, Caunt rushed his rival into the ropes and floored him with a mighty right-hander to the chin. Big Ben walked back to his corner thinking the round was over, but Bendy had bounced to his feet and was tearing after him. Caunt's seconds yelled a warning and he dropped to his haunches as a precautionary measure. Immediately a great shout went up of 'foul' and poor Ben had lost again, Bendy's friends having to protect him from the fury of those who had lost their money.

After that he beat Tom Paddock in forty rounds by the now familiar method of getting his opponent disqualified and then retired. His stalwart mother had died and Bendy went all to pieces, spending most of his time in Nottingham jail on charges of drunkenness and disorderly conduct. After 38 convictions he reformed and became an evangelist. Meeting Lord Longford in London one day he explained that he had given up the ring and was now fighting the Devil. 'Well,' came the reply, 'I trust you are treating him a lot more fairly than you did poor Ben Caunt.' Running downstairs at his home at the age of 69, Bendigo tripped and fell, breaking three ribs, one of which penetrated a lung, causing his death. And so that he should never be forgotten the people of Nottingham erected a massive memorial to him.

18

From the Bread-Line to the Title

James J. Braddock

I wonder if Jim Braddock would have won the heavyweight championship of the world if he had not been a married man with three children. His chance came at a time when his spirits were at their lowest, his financial resources nil and his debts mounting. It came when he had been out of the ring for nine months and in the eyes of the fight fraternity was a worn-out, washed-up boxer. Braddock's is the story that reads more like fiction than fact. No doubt he sometimes wonders if it wasn't all a lovely dream.

His parents came from Manchester, yet they did not meet and marry until both had been living in America for some time. They set up home in the rugged section of New York known as 'Hell's Kitchen' and produced a brood of seven, two girls and five boys. Last but one in the order of arrival was a lusty son whom they named James Joseph. Every boy had to know how to fight in that quarter of the big city and those who were best at it quickly turned it to profit. Jimmy followed his older brothers into the local boxing club and then into the paid amateurs. In three years he had 45 bouts, winning thirty of them inside the distance.

The family moved into New Jersey and there, at the age of 18, Jimmy turned professional. He made great strides and showed every promise of developing into a top ranker. One of his brothers, Joey, gave up the ring to manage the youngster, but passed him over to Joe Gould, an experienced handler of fighters, when Jimmy gave signs of becoming a contender for the light-heavyweight title. Gould was an aggressive little man who knew how to get the best out of a fighter and secure the highest purses. They formed a lasting partnership that saw them through thick and thin and finally to prosperity.

Braddock's speciality was a chilling right-hand punch that could knock a man down and out. Jimmy pawed with his left until he saw an opening for a swift right. And if this landed in the nerve territory of a rival's jaw, he could start pulling off his gloves. But a persistent right-hand puncher of power can come unstuck sometimes. Jimmy drove it hard at a coloured fighter's head one night, heard an ominous click, felt an electric shock pass up his arm and knew he had broken his best weapon.

He let it heal of its own accord, but it pained him so much when he resumed fighting that he had to see a specialist. The bone had knitted badly and would have to be broken again and reset. Braddock was ready for that until he heard how much it would cost. 'I can break it myself and earn dough doing it,' he snorted. He accomplished this piece of do-it-yourself surgery in his next contest, the broken bones were re-set and the career continued. But now, instinctively, Braddock was shy of tossing his right with all its old-time freedom, so more of his opponents were able to stay the distance, a fact that lost him a lot of fan appeal, and the interest of promoters.

Even so, he was good enough to fight his way into the role of light-heavyweight challenger, meeting Tommy Loughran for the title at the New York Yankee Stadium. He got the licking of his life. Loughran was no puncher, but an immaculate fencer, with excellent ringcraft and boxing skill. He won each of the fifteen rounds and sent Braddock back to New Jersey looking very much the worse for wear.

It was a decidedly dismal Jimmy who made his way round to his girl-friend's home the following Saturday night. She was Mae Theresa Fox, a telephone operator, and her brother, a buddy of Braddock's, had often brought him home to supper. James thought the world of Mae, but could never summon up enough pluck to ask her to marry him. They went out regularly and she waited patiently for him to propose. But the fighter, who never had much to say for himself at any time, was practically struck dumb in her presence.

She looked at his puffed-up eyes and bruised cheeks, the

work of Loughran's artistry, and felt terribly sorry for him. Jimmy mumbled something through his battered lips and although she couldn't catch what he said, she made a wild and hopeful guess. 'Yes, I'll marry you, Jim, and don't let us wait too long.' She kissed him and sent him home with the surprised thought that somehow he had become engaged.

Mae was so thrilled she even promised to see his next fight in New York, a great concession, because up to now she had resisted all his entreaties to watch him box. Now they both wished she hadn't. He was meeting Maxie Rosenbloom, notorious slapper and slapstick performer. The crafty old veteran boxed Jimmy's ears off and after five rounds Mae could not stand any more and ran out of the building.

Next time they met they had a serious talk. She wanted to know if he had enough money to give up the Fight Game and get married straight away. Braddock had 30,000 dollars saved, most of it in stocks and bonds, some in a taxi-cab business. It was agreed that they should set up home as soon as he had got through the fights Joe Gould had on hand for him. After that he would quit boxing and devote his whole time to the taxi-cabs.

Joe Gould was quite agreeable and asked if they had fixed a date for the wedding. Braddock told him it would be January 18th, but was reminded that he would be fighting Leo Lomski at Chicago the night before. James pleaded that it just wasn't possible. He might get a black eye and Mae would be real mad if he turned up at the church with one. 'I can't postpone the fight because of a wedding,' snapped Gould. 'You're getting six grand and a third of that is mine, whereas you're getting all the dame to yourself.' He hung up. When Jimmy told Miss Fox she agreed to a week's postponement and no more. He lost to Lomski, they got married and although it was a happy venture, it was not a lucky one.

America was in the thick of a deep economic depression. Jim's stocks fell to zero, he had to sell his share in the taxi-cab business to pay his way. They started a family and got into debt. One morning he went round to see Joe Gould. 'I have been waiting for you to show up,' said the manager. 'It means a fresh start, but I have got friends. Get yourself into shape and I'll call you.'

Mae wasn't pleased, but she knew it was inevitable. In the next three years Braddock had 24 bouts and lost 13 of them. From the top of the ratings he slipped into the second-class heavyweight ranks. The end came when he smashed up his right hand again. An examination proved that it would take six months to repair, so Jim needed a job to keep going. There were three children now, Jay, Howard and Rose Marie, a big responsibility for an unskilled out-of-work.

He tried the docks, the railways, the roads. He got temporary work and even this dwindled. By Christmas 1933 he was on relief, receiving about eight dollars a week to keep the five of them. He owed a milk bill of 35 dollars and the kids needed milk more than anything. The dairyman stopped delivering and in desperation Braddock sought out Joe Gould again. He found him at Madison Square Garden. Gould did not have 35 dollars, he too was having a lean time. He borrowed the money from Jimmy Johnston, matchmaker to the Garden, and Braddock hastened off to pay his most important debt.

In the next six months things went from bad to worse. Braddock did any job the labour exchange could find for him. His damaged hand was a great handicap and he used his left to do the bulk of his lifting and hammering. To add to his meagre income, he engaged himself as sparring-partner to the leading heavies, using his left to keep them at bay. How he wished he had used it more in his fighting days.

The phone rang in Gould's one room office. It was Johnston on the line. Hastily little Joe started to say that he had not forgotten the 35 dollars he had borrowed on Braddock's behalf, but the Garden matchmaker was not thinking of such chicken feed. One of his fighters in a forthcoming contest had broken down in training and a substitute was urgently required. Johnston wanted to know if Braddock was fit enough to take the fight. Gould assured him that Jimmy was always in good shape and would jump at the chance. How much could he expect for his services?

'I can offer him 250 to fight this new boy Corn Griffin,' went on Johnston. 'But he's got to stay a few rounds.' 'Griffin is a puncher,' pointed out the manager. 'He knocks them all out and he has not been beaten yet. Can't you give us something a bit easier, Jimmy?' 'Griffin or nothing,' came the reply, so Griffin it was and Gould impressed on his boxer that it was imperative that he should remain in the ring for as long as possible. Overjoyed at getting another contest Braddock quietly assured his manager that he would not let anyone down. He kept his word. Inside three rounds he had punched Griffin into obscurity, the referee stopping a contest that had been one-sided from the start.

'You weren't supposed to do that,' complained Johnston in the dressing-room. 'So now you fight John Henry Lewis, and this time stay in your place.' Braddock licked Lewis so decisively that the critics, who had given him no chance of beating Griffin and even less of beating Lewis, now began to think of him in terms of a heavyweight championship contender.

One man stood in the way. Number one challenger Art Lasky. Johnston paired him with Braddock in a final eliminator and the 29-year old Jimmy stunned them by turning in another superb victory, a master-versus-pupil exhibition of sound left-hand boxing. The result upset all calculations. 'You can't put Braddock in with Max Baer,' everyone told the Garden matchmaker. 'It will be sheer murder.' Baer had floored Primo Carnera eleven times to win the world title, he had just knocked out King Levinsky with one punch. He had been partly responsible for the death of two men. His right-hand punching was devastating.

Johnston hesitated, but Gould would not let him off the hook. He had advertised the fight with Lasky as being a final stepping-stone to a title bout and he would create an uproar if Braddock did not get his chance. 'It won't draw a dime,' wailed the matchmaker. 'They won't bet on who will win, but how long Braddock will last.' The boxing writers to a man said it was no match. After a month they had not sold a ticket. Then someone – and I'll let you guess who – whispered in a boxing writer's ear that Braddock had come straight off the relief line to fight for the championship.

It wasn't exactly true, but it was a hell of a story. Jimmy, in fact, had paid one visit to the relief office since his victory over Griffin and that was to pay back the 300 dollars he had drawn in the nine months he had been out of work. But the fans lapped it up. They called Braddock the 'Cinderella Man', there were pictures of Mae and the kids and heartbreak stories of the family sufferings. They piled it on so thick that 35,000 flocked into the Garden Bowl on Long Island to see the head of the Braddock family sacrifice himself for his loved ones.

Ha! Ha! Ha! You don't have to be told that Jimmy boxed rings round the big bad Baer, stabbed him to abject defeat with a stiff, straight left, easily avoided his efforts to land a big punch, and walked off with a unanimous verdict after starting a 10-to-1 underdog in the betting. After ten long and despairing years he had become heavyweight champion of the world. 'To what do you attribute your success?' someone asked him in the crowded dressing-room after the biggest upset in years. 'Opening the door and finding no milk on the step,' answered Jimmy.

Things were a lot different from then on; there were a lot of fringe benefits available to a heavyweight king. But he was coming up to his thirtieth birthday and at that age he could not expect a long reign. Mae realised that only too well, so did Joe Gould. Together they planned that Jimmy would earn as much as he could with newspaper and magazine stories, public appearances, advertising goods and whatever might come his way. Fortunately there was no outstanding challenger knocking on the championship door and Braddock did not intend to go looking for one. A 21-year old coloured lad from Alabama was coming along rapidly and while he was on his way to the top the Braddocks would reap the biggest harvest available. Their plans were heightened when Max Schmeling caused a sensation by knocking out the up-and-coming Joe Louis.

This was in the summer of 1936 and the German's unexpected success was both a shock and a setback to Promoter Mike Jacobs' plans. Schmeling automatically became the leading contender for Braddock's title, but because of what was going on in his country under the Nazi regime, every effort was made to avoid such a match. Jimmy was prepared to meet Schmeling and the New York Boxing Commission ordered the contest to take place. Jacobs, however, wanted Louis in the challenger's corner. Since his defeat by Schmeling, Joe had made a triumphant comeback with seven successive wins and the promoter planned to put the fight on in Chicago.

Husband, wife and manager put their heads together and decided that if Uncle Mike wanted them to flout the New York authorities, he would have to make it worthwhile. The promoter had to agree that the champion would receive fifty per cent of the gate receipts at Comiskey Park, Chicago's baseball stadium, which incidentally provided Jimmy with 293,660 dollars, more than he had earned in all his ten years of fighting, plus an off-the-record bonus of ten per cent of all Louis' earnings in the event of the championship changing hands. As Louis defended his title no less than 25 times, the Braddocks did very well for themselves.

Jimmy stayed eight rounds with the Brown Bomber whom he put on the canvas with a cute punch in the opening round and it was exhaustion more than punishment that finally caused his defeat. That he was not demoralised by being knocked out was evidenced seven months later when he surprisingly outpointed the far younger Tommy Farr over ten rounds in New York. He wanted to retire on a winning note. After that, his wife did not have too difficult a job in inducing him to hang up his gloves for good.

19

Grandma Made Him Pray for Victory

Rocky Graziano

There were three important women in the turbulent fighting life of Rocky Graziano, middleweight champion of the world. His wife, his mother and his grandmother and each played a big part in changing a city roughneck into a respectable citizen. Born Rocco Barbella, in New York's notorious East Side, he started life filled with hate. He loathed his cold-water tenement home; he despised his father, an ex-boxer of small account, for forcing him to box with his older and bigger brother who aspired to making a name for himself in the professional ring.

Rocky disliked school and all forms of discipline; he disapproved of the rules that govern society. He hated the cops who enforced the law and had no time for his law-abiding neighbours. Above all, he had an inborn disgust for the fact the family was poverty-stricken. He loved freedom and spent most of his time on the roof-tops away from the hurly-burly of the packed and noisy streets. But to be free you need money, so when hunger brought him down, he stole – anything he could lay his hands on.

His first arrest came at the tender age of ten when he and another boy were caught raiding the slot machines in the subway. It was his grandmother who spoke for him at the childrens' court and took him to her own place away from the over-crowded Barbella home. But if she thought she might be a restraining influence on his wild nature, she was mistaken. She was to stand security for him on many more occasions as he grew older and more venturesome.

Eventually he was sent up for theft and violence, and Grandma had to leave him in the care of the prison authorities.

Disappointed she realised that he was heading straight for Sing Sing, even to the electric chair. There were terms of probation, then parole, but once free he resumed his wild life unhesitatingly. He became a gang leader, a marked man. It got to the point where the police were waiting for him to become an adult so that he could be given the full corrective treatment.

During one of the periods of freedom, which got shorter each time, his pals kidded him into taking a bout in the State Amateur Championships because the only Brooklyn entry had dropped out. Rocky wasn't keen. He·was always ready to swap punches in the street, provided he got in the first swipe, but doing it for sport he considered cissy. Even the promise of a gold watch if he won did not appeal. All he wanted to know was how much it would fetch in a pawnshop.

He was told that it had prestige value, information that merely made Rocky snort with disgust. But he went in, won his heat, then another, and finally took the title, his fierce fighting and savage punching causing a sensation. Lupo the Wolf was waiting when he came out of the arena juggling the watch in his big hand. He took the youngster into a nearby billiards hall and they had an earnest conversation, during which Rocky parted with his prize for ten dollars and learned how to make money at boxing while he was too young to obtain a professional licence. He could engage in two or three bouts a week in the many amateur clubs in the district, with little chance of suffering defeat because of his hard-hitting prowess. His promoter had an arrangement by which he sold the watches back to the various club secretaries, so there was no risk of a young boxer losing his unpaid status. When he was old enough to fight for money he would be sufficiently experienced to start earning dollars by the fistfull.

Rocky listened and nodded his head approvingly. This put a different slant on boxing. He was taken from one so-called amateur show to another and he was sensational. He liked slamming into other guys and found it easy to pick up twenty or thirty dollars a week. Sometimes he took a licking, but not often. When he came home with a swollen face, a jagged cut or a closed-up eye, his mother cried. She implored him not to become a fighter, pointing out what the profession had done for his father. She urged him to settle down, get himself a regular job, find a nice girl and make her proud of him.

Grandma had the same idea, but he listened to neither of them. When he wasn't boxing he was out with the gang. One day he was picked up for a break-in he knew nothing about and his fighting career came to an abrupt end. While he was serving the sentence his mother came to see him. She said it was her third visit and that she had been refused permission on the previous occasions. With a big grin he told her that he wasn't surprised; that he had been in solitary confinement for assaulting a prison officer. Proudly he boasted that he was giving the authorities more trouble than any other inmate.

She looked at him with troubled eyes and then made a bold decision. It was not time for her to go, but she got up. If that was his attitude there was no sense in remaining any longer. She was ashamed of him and told him so, adding that she never wished to see him again. When she had gone Rocky was shaken. When his grandma also stayed away, he was shattered. From then on he behaved so well the prison officials could not believe it. He served out his time and ran all the way home.

He greeted his mother affectionately, he visited his grandmother, then he went looking for the boys. There were none about. Suddenly it occurred to him that there was a war on in Europe and those of his pals who were not in jail or hadn't been killed in gang fights were in the forces. He had never felt so lonely in his life. He walked round the streets. Passing Lou Stillman's famous gymnasium on Broadway, he retraced his steps and walked in. Once before he had been there for a trial bout, and knocked out a sparring-partner in twenty seconds. They hadn't forgotten him and were suitably impressed when he announced that he was ready to become a paid fighter. Irving Cohen, a reputable boxers' manager, agreed to take him in hand; before he could get started Rocky was inducted into national service.

He spent most of his short Army life in the glass house. He was a pain in the neck to the officers. Finally, he slugged one journey he evaded his guard and slipped off the train and made his way back to Stillman's Gym. He contacted Manager Cohen, told him he had been discharged, changed his name to Graziano and had half-a-dozen sizzling contests before the M.P.s caught up with him as he sat in a dressing-room waiting to go on. 'I'll come after the fight,' he told them blandly. But he went immediately and suffered incarceration for being absent without leave, which was added to the sentence he received from his interrupted court-martial.

It seemed that his boxing career was suspended for the duration, but eventually Uncle Sam decided he could win the war quicker without Rocky's help; he was given a dishonourable discharge. Then began a most amazing rise to fistic fame. Graziano flattened one opponent after another. He hit them so hard they went out with the first big punch he could land. If they messed him about with some scientific stuff, he grabbed them with his left and pulled them into socking rights until they were rendered unconscious. He had little defence, but a rock-like chin and the capacity to come back from a shattering blow and crash in a return shot that was even harder.

He made plenty of money and, to his great joy, was making it legitimately. He moved his mother into a better apartment. He bought clothes for his brother and sisters and provided Grandma with some of life's comforts. He helped out old friends who were in need, but kept away from the gang. Then he met Norma Unger, a quiet, good-looking Jewish girl from the better-class district of Ocean Park. She was a friend of his sister Yolande and he fell for her on sight.

Everything was thrown overboard. He neglected his training to take her out; he even forgot to attend the weigh-in for a fight. He and his manager were called before the Boxing Commission; Rocky blurted out that his breach of the regulations was due to the fact that he had found a girl friend. The Chairman advised him to marry without delay if he wished to keep his boxing licence, which was just the sort of advice that Graziano needed. He and Norma were married that week. She brought him into her part of New York and did not encourage him to bring home his former disreputable friends. She taught him to wear a collar and tie, and to have a suit instead of the sweat-shirt and tight pants that he was fond of running around in. Slowly she put respectability into Rocky.

Fortunately this grooming had no effect on the ferocity of his fighting. Once in the ring, he clenched his iron fists and became a destructive puncher with the sole idea of battering the opposition into pulp. The fans hadn't seen anything like it for years. They packed in to watch Graziano go snarling into action. They marvelled at his durability and the savage way he fought regardless of the rules. Referees seemed to be spellbound at the ferocity of his fighting. Soon there were only the rated boxers to match him with and he beat them up one after the other.

He ruined two welterweight champions, first Freddie Cochrane who was stopped twice in ten rounds, then Marty Servo, whose nose he broke and battered so severely that he had to turn down a 60,000 dollar guarantee to defend his title against Sugar Ray Robinson – in fact he was forced to retire altogether from boxing. He flattened Billy Arnold, Al Davis and Harold Green, victories that brought him right up to the middleweight king. Tony Zale was a knockout specialist in his own right, as hard as the steel they made in his home-town of Gary, Indiana. He had won his last six contests in a grand total of 22 rounds. Although he had not been long out of the U.S. Navy, he had soon got back into his fighting stride.

Graziano made his championship challenge in the Yankee Stadium in New York before 39,827 eager spectators who paid 342,497 dollars and saw the battle of a lifetime for their money. Here were two vigorous sluggers who could take as well as give, and there was no finessing. Rocky was out to batter the champion into helplessness with all speed; Zale was there to knock this dangerous opponent kicking on the canvas.

Fists flew, big punches, each meant to be a finisher. Zale got there first, a flashing left hook that put Rocky on his pants, the most surprised person in the big city. He sprang up and tore into Tony, who measured him with a telling right to the chin. Graziano rode the punch well and tossed back a vicious counter. Reporters lost count of the mighty blows that were given and taken in that explosive first round, but there was a lot more to come.

The second round was just as tempestuous, each being rocked in turn. Then Graziano got through with another of his deadly rights to the jaw and Zale was sent flat on his back. The crowd roared with excitement. It looked as though a new champion was about to be crowned. But the bell saved Zale, he made an amazing recovery in the minute interval to come up fresh for the third to continue this wild war that was thrilling the fight-crazy spectators.

Rocky threw more punches than ever before, but Zale was the faster hitter, his blows thudding into the challenger while he rode most of Rocky's big bombs. They kept the pace going and the punishment absorbed on both sides was unbelievable. Having nailed his rival with another dynamic right in the fifth round, Rocky returned to his corner to tell them it would be all over in the next, that the champ was going weak and could not last much longer. Soon after the start of the next round a fierce right sent Zale back on his heels. He flashed back and missed and Graziano stormed in, his big right cocked for the payoff punch. He roared and rushed in for the 'kill'.

A million stars lit up in his brain. The ring floor came up with a rush and hit him full in the face. Rocky rolled over, grabbed at the nearby ropes and sat there facing the fans, unable to move his legs and get to his feet. He was counted out and he could not believe it. When they told him in the corner that it was all over, that he had failed to win the championship, he was broken-hearted. Even the knowledge that he had earned nearly 80,000 dollars did not console him. He went home by himself.

Norma had waited up and was all tenderness and sympathy. For a week she gave herself up to his comfort, encouraging him to realise that defeat was not the end of everything. His old mob had the same idea. Three of them called round one evening and Rocky asked them in, but they wanted to speak to him in the hall. They were planning a break-in at a factory and wanted his help. All he was required to do was to take care of the night-watchman. It promised to be a very profitable venture and there would be a worthwhile share for each of them.

When Graziano refused to have any part of the proposed robbery they became very angry and accused him of ratting on his friends. He explained that he now had a high position in the Fight Game; because of the great showing he had made against Zale he was still the leading contender for the title; as far as he was concerned the old days were over for good. He asked them to go. They grew nasty. One drew a knife. Rocky clenched his big fists. Another slid a hand towards his arm-pit. The sitting-room door opened and there stood Norma. Quietly she asked them to leave, reiterating what her husband had told them; that he had finished with his old life and was not going back to crime. They looked menacingly at her, but when she informed them that she had already 'phoned the police, she and Rocky watched them scuttling down the stairs and out into a waiting car.

Contracts were signed for the return fight with Zale, but Graziano needed a tune-up bout before going into full training and it was arranged that he should box a second-rate middle named Reuben Shank, a former cowboy from Keensburg, Colorado, who seemed a pretty harmless opponent, having lost his last five contests. They made Rocky a hot favourite to win. During a work-out in the gymnasium, however, Graziano pulled a shoulder muscle and it was decided to cancel the contest. Rocky went home and a few days later was surprised to find himself ordered to appear before the District Attorney.

To his amazement he was accused of having agreed to lose to Shank so that gangsters could make a killing at the expense of the bookmakers, who would likewise clean-up on the fight fans. It was alleged that Graziano had accepted a bribe to 'lay down', but had later thought better of it and faked the shoulder injury in order to put himself in the clear. Rocky denied these allegations, but did not help his cause when, during his interrogation, he blurted out that he had been approached to 'throw' fights on many occasions; that such happenings were all part of the fight scene. An enquiry by the New York State Boxing Commission followed and although Rocky was cleared of all charges, his licence was revoked.

So the second fight with Zale had to be taken into the Chicago Stadium. It was ten months after their first brawl and although the indoor attendance was reduced to 18,547 fans, the receipts reached 422,009 dollars, everyone anticipating a repeat performance of their New York slugfest. After the weigh-in ceremony, Rocky was moving off to go back to his hotel for a meal and a rest before going to the arena, when an old lady elbowed her way through the crowd and took hold of his arm. It was Grandma. 'You are coming with me,' she ordered and the scowling world-title contender allowed himself to be taken into a nearby church. They went to a front pew and she made him kneel beside her and pray for victory, pointing out that he had been on his own last time, but now they would see if the Lord would help him.

The fight that night was as torrid as the first. In the opening round Zale crashed home a right that split Graziano's left eyebrow wide open. In the second, he short-stabbed Rocky with head punches, sizzling shots that came too fast for his challenger to dodge. Obviously the champion was out for-a quick win, and in the third he belted the Brooklyn boy with a right to the jaw that dropped him in a heap. And when Graziano got up he was pounded non-stop until it looked as though he must be knocked out.

Rocky went through the fourth and fifth rounds in a complete daze, and at the bell the referee came to his corner and looked at his savaged eye. The bleeding had been stopped, but it was as big as an egg. Obviously, one more punch would burst it assunder. Rocky pleaded with the official not to stop the bout and was told he could come out for just one more round. Into it he packed all the fighting savagery he knew, all the venom, the last remains of his strength and energy. Zale was a mere blur before him, a dancing red shadow. Rocky could not feel the punches any more, he was throwing his own from both hands, he could not stop punching. Suddenly he felt a smart slap across his face, a dozen hands seemed to be holding down his arms. He was dragged back into his corner. 'It's all over,' they yelled at him. 'You've stopped him. You punched him into helplessness on the ropes. You're the new champion of the world.'

Next day he rode through Brooklyn in an open car, a large plaster over his left eye, a smile a mile wide and his arm round Norma's waist. The crowds were cheering, the cops were waving. He was one of their own, a respected citizen and a hero. Rocky Graziano had knocked out the notorious Rocco Barbella, the hoodlum, the bum.

There was the usual return-fight clause in the contract which called upon Graziano to meet Zale again within ninety days, but more than a year passed before they could have their rubber meeting. Rocky was still without a licence to box in New York and now he was suffering a complete ban in the State of Illinois because a Chicago newspaper had launched a campaign against a former criminal with a dishonourable discharge from the U.S. Army being allowed to fight for a world boxing title. Even when he engaged in a ten-round contest for a single dollar purse in a charity tournament, the fistic powers would not relent.

Eventually Graziano and Zale had their third fight at Ruppert's Stadium at Newark, in the State of New Jersey; despite the long period of time that had elapsed, the interest in them had not flagged. 21,497 spectators marched through the turnstiles to the tune of 335,646 dollars, with a further 70,000 dollars coming from film and radio rights. Zale had engaged in three bouts since losing his title, winning all of them inside the scheduled distance, whereas Graziano had engaged in the solitary charity contest and was worried by the adverse publicity he had received since becoming champion.

All the savagery had been burned out of him in those first two fights with the man from the Steel City, all his keen enthusiasm had been sapped by his troubles outside the ring. His training had become a chore rather than an exciting run-up to a long-awaited event. Of more significance, life with Norma had gradually tamed him. She had taught him to have some regard for the feelings of others, to act like a human being when he was out of the ring. In doing so, she had destroyed his natural lust for physical domination.

They swapped punches as before, they pounded each other freely and fiercely, but it was Zale's blows that carried the most dynamite and mid-way through round three a left hook crashed against Rocky's one-time armour-plated jaw and stretched him out flat on the canvas for the full count. After they brought him home, he locked the door, took the telephone off its hook and talked to no one but Norma for a month. A year later he was induced to make the inevitable comeback. Although scoring a number of victories that looked good in the record book, he was no match for Sugar Ray Robinson. He was stopped in three rounds, to bring his colourful career to a dramatic close.

Jack Dempsey with promoter Tex Rickard at the Lincoln Fields training camp. Left to right: Estelle Taylor Dempsey, Dempsey (holding Maxine Rickard), Mrs Rickard and Rickard

Below left: Jack Dempsey and Jack 'Doc' Kearns in 1950 when they met to forget the past

Below right: John C. Heenan, 'The Benicia Boy'. A print of 1858

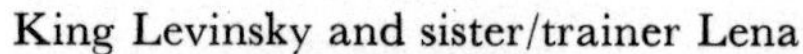

Adah Isaacs Menken, John C. Heenan's wife, as 'The Naked Lady'

King Levinsky and sister/trainer Lena

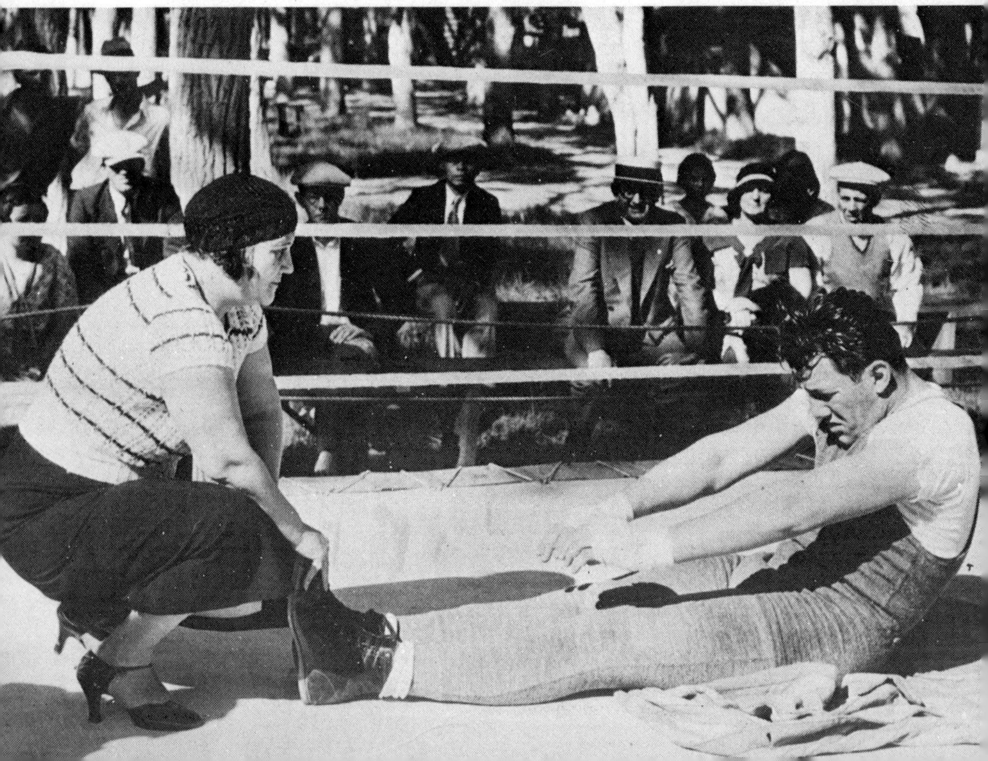

Stanley Ketchel (left) swinging at Jack Johnson, before the coloured champion knocked him out. 16 October 1909

Below: Jack Johnson with his mother and third wife Lucille Cameron

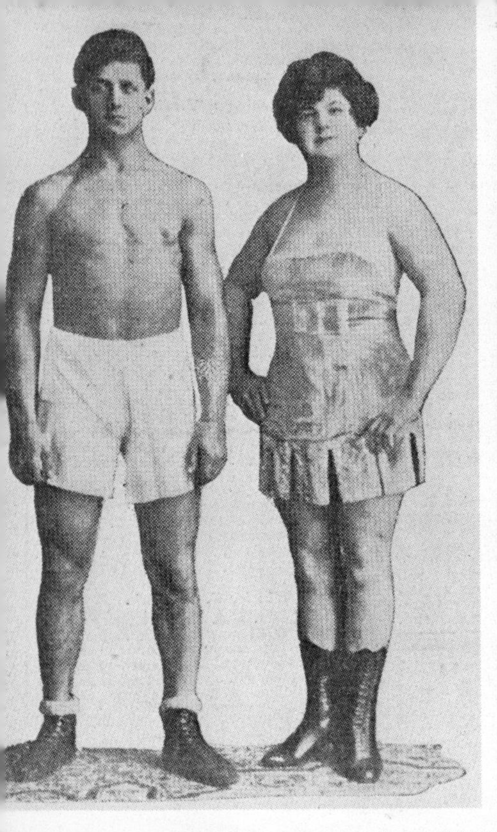

TED SANDWINA

Above left: Ted Sandwina with his mother Kati, 'The Strongest Woman in the World'

Above right: A fighting pose by Sandwina

Left: John Lawrence Sullivan at the start of his career

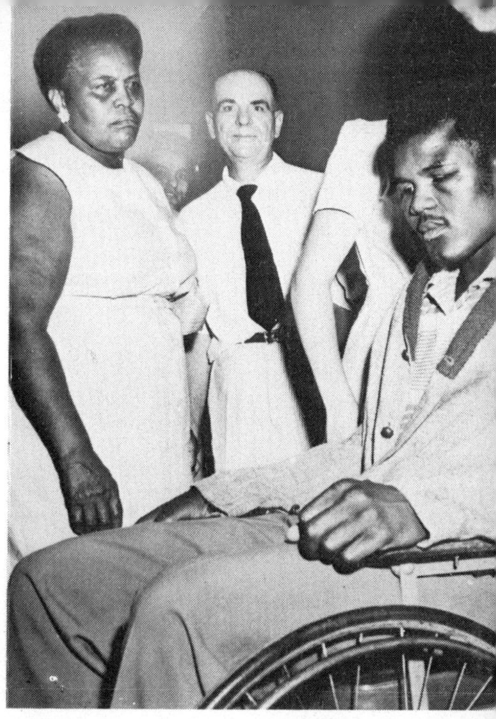

Left: Floyd Patterson flooring Tommy Jackson in the first round of the title fight which ended in the tenth. 29 July 1957

Right: Jackson visited by his mother in hospital after the fight

Jimmy Wilde in training, paced by his wife. 1918

Above right: Mrs Cook – manager for George Cook

Above left: George Cook (left) attacking giant Frank Goddard. Cook won on points over twenty rounds

Left: Jack Doyle with Mexican film star Movita Castenada who became his second wife

Randolph Turpin loses on points to Carl (Bobo) Olson: down in the ninth. 24 October 1953, when they fought for the vacant world middleweight title

Randolph Turpin with wife Gwenneth Price at Harringay shortly after their marriage. 8 December 1953

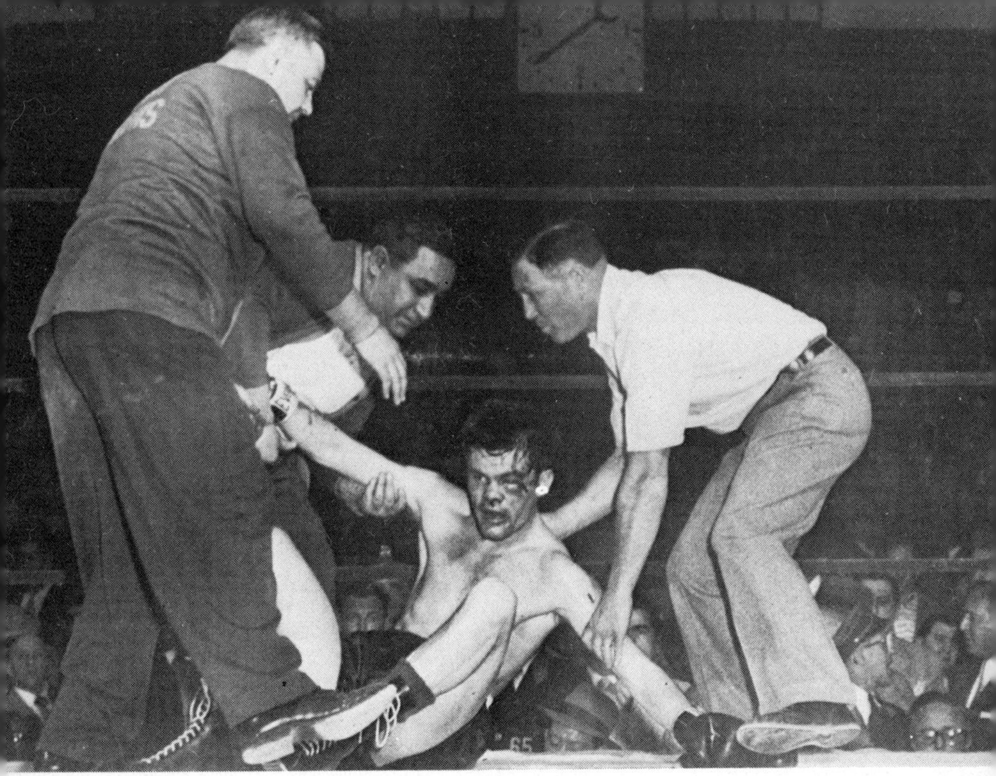

Referee Tommy Rawson helps Tommy Collins, after the tenth knockdown in the lightweight title fight Collins lost to Jimmy Carter. 24 April 1953

Collins, Tommy Collins Jr, and Mrs Collins – the day after

Lew Jenkins puts Lou Ambers through the ropes prior to stopping him in the third to win the world lightweight title. 10 May 1940

Katie Jenkins seconding Carmine Fatta in Brooklyn. 30 June 1944

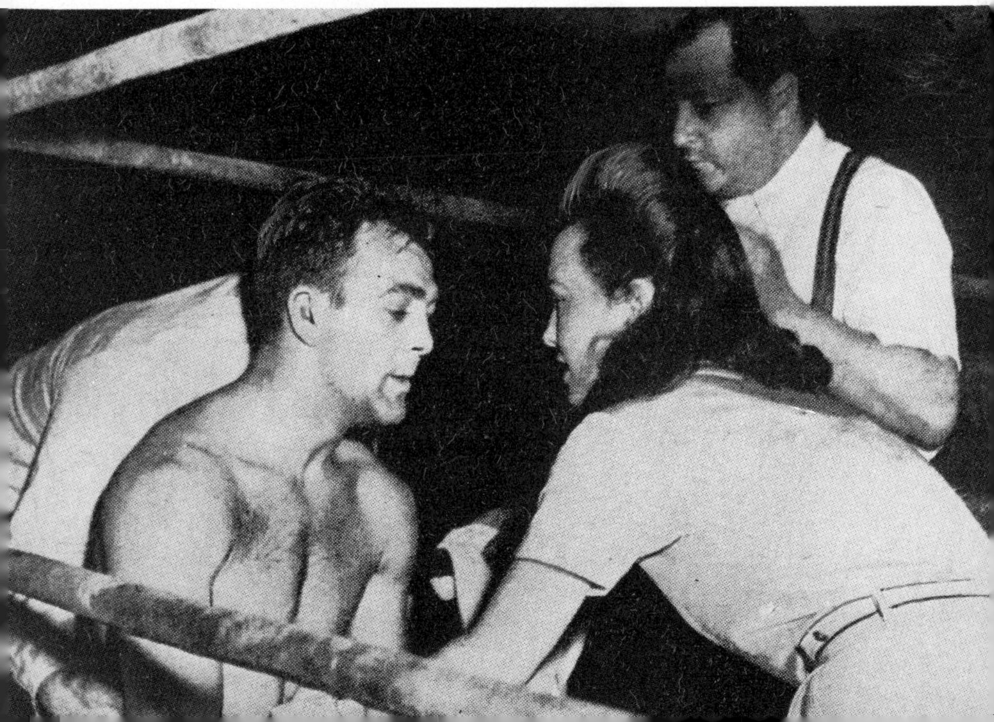

The end of the contest between Bold Bendigo and Tom Paddock, when the latter was disqualified in the forty-ninth round. 5 June 1840

Middleweight Champion Rocky Graziano in his Brooklyn home, with wife Norma (right), mother-in-law (left), grandmother, and daughter Audrey in his arms

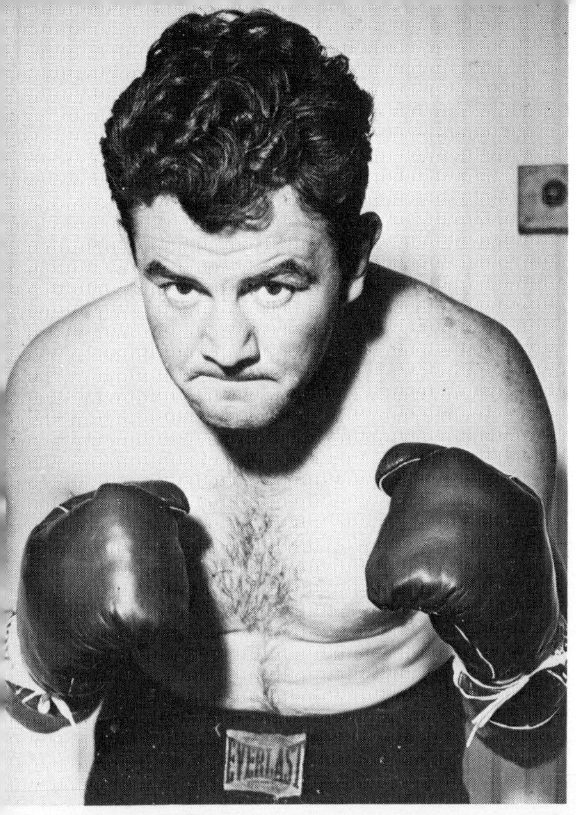

James J. Braddock, World Heavy-weight Champion 1935-7

Below: Though bleeding, Rocky Graziano moves in on Charlie Fusari; he went on to win on a technical knockout in the tenth round

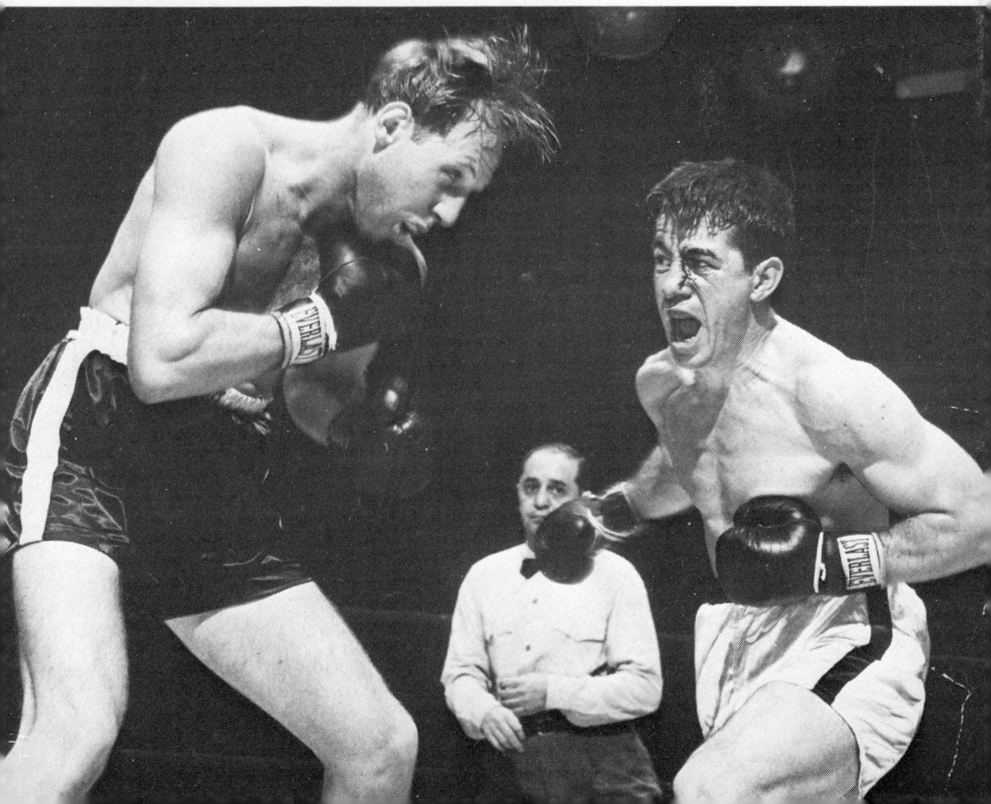

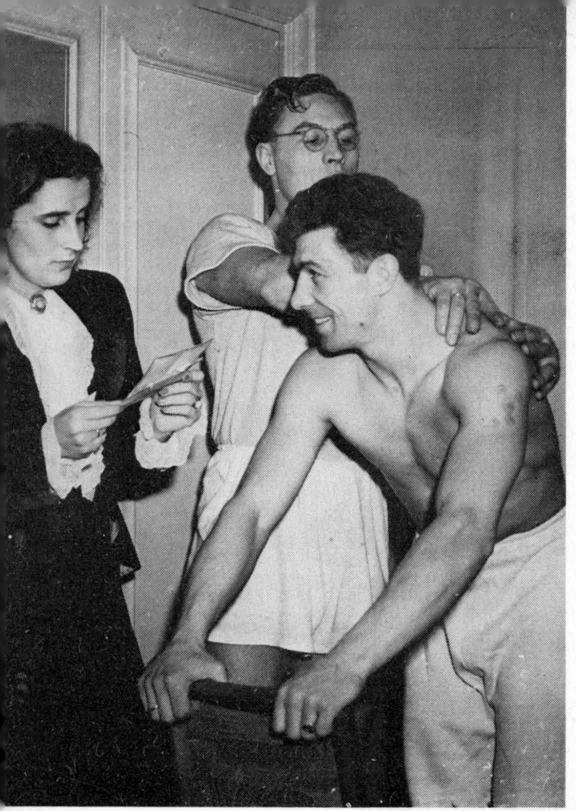

Left: Mrs Luc van Dam reads good-luck telegrams to her husband, prior to his meeting Albert Finch at the Albert Hall. 24 January 1949

Joe Louis at his training camp at Lakewood, New Jersey, with first wife Marva Trotter

Above: Ingemar Johansson and family arrive in New York for his title fight with Floyd Patterson. Left to right: Jens (father), Annette (brother Rolf's fiancée), Rolf, Brigit Lundgren (Ingemar's fiancée), Eva (sister), Ebba (mother) and Henry (brother)

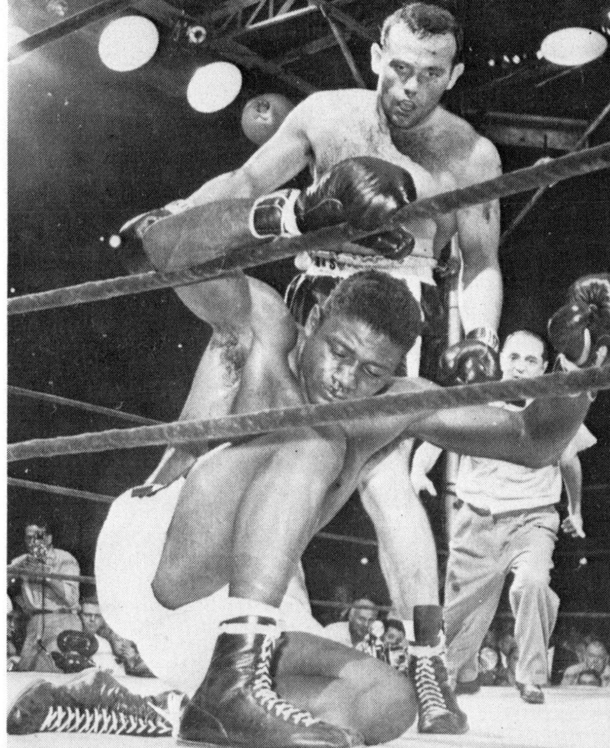

Right: Floyd Patterson down for the seventh time in the first fight with Johansson which the Swede won in three rounds

Jersey Joe Walcott, his wife Lydia, and their six children – the day after he lost on points to Joe Louis. 5 December 1947

Sugar Ray Robinson stops Randolph Turpin (right). New York 1951

Ray Robinson in a typical
boxing stance

Edna Mae, Robinson's wife, at
the fight with Jake LaMotta:
Sugar Ray Robinson won by a
technical knockout in the
thirteenth to become World
Middleweight Champion

Cassius Clay (Muhammad Ali) crashes to the canvas in the fourth round of his fight with Henry Cooper. The fight was stopped in Clay's favour in the fifth because of Cooper's badly cut eye. 18 June 1963

Henry Cooper and twin brother Jim help their mother Mrs Lily Cooper

20

Manager-Wife Made Calamitous Mis-Match

Luc van Dam

Most promoters, and almost every boxers' manager, abhor wives who interfere with the fighting careers of their husbands. They complain that when a boxer is single he is easy enough to handle, but once he is wed, all sorts of complications arise, principally due to the influence exerted by the fair newcomer into the act. The wives of fighting men have a reputation for being dissatisfied with any purse that is offered, no matter how large; they also resent the traditional percentage deducted by the manager. More than one has pressed her husband to look after his own affairs and when he has confessed his inability to do so, she has taken on the job herself, sometimes with disastrous results.

With a large family and the urgent need for a bigger home, Mrs Lucien van Dam might be excused for taking charge. For a time she did wonderfully well, then she aimed a little too high for her husband and brought him down with a resounding crash. Susan was no dumb blonde, but a lovely brunette, with glistening jet-black hair tumbling to her shoulders, beautifully cut features, a pair of wonderful eyes, a figure to turn back and look at, and she also had plenty of intelligence.

German-born, and a refugee from the Nazis, she had found shelter in Holland with the van Dam family. During the war she spent most of her time hidden in the house, and no one was astonished when Lucien announced his intention of marrying her. For some while she took little interest in his boxing career, as her freedom was in constant peril, but when Lucien had been fighting professionally for ten years without getting anywhere beyond the championship of his country, and they had been married long enough to produce three delightful children – Biana, Eddie and Susy – she thought it was high time they retained in the family the usual managerial cut in her husband's earnings.

Lucien could see no objection provided Susan pulled her weight. So while he did his roadwork, she paced him on a bicycle and in the gym she held the watch as he went through his sparring, bag-punching and calisthenics. In addition, she bargained with promoters, dealt with the correspondence and autographed his fan photos for him. Under her influence van Dam became a man of substance in the middleweight division. Promoters from outside Holland began to seek his services.

For some time everything went according to plan and Susan was certainly justifying her position, then she got it into her pretty head that her husband could beat the best in the world. And there was certain justification for this belief, apart from the understandable and unshakable faith she had in her husband's fistic ability. At that time Luc was at his very peak, a sound box-fighter of experience and considerable talent.

Born in Rotterdam in 1920, he came of a well-known fighting family, having a number of brothers who had made names for themselves as outstanding amateurs. It was therefore only natural that he would be prompted to follow suit. He proved to be the best of the bunch, and so far superior to the other Dutch lads at his weight that they breathed a sigh of relief when he elected to turn professional soon after his eighteenth birthday.

There had been another reason to inspire this move. Employed as a furniture remover, he installed a particularly fine bedroom suite one morning, stepped back to admire his handiwork and fell through an open window into the street. He should have been killed, but when he picked himself up and found he was unhurt, he decided that boxing for a living could not be more hazardous, so found himself a manager and entered the paid ranks.

The war and the invasion of his country by the Germans gave Lucien an opportunity to exploit his fighting instincts with resistance work. This kept him fit, inventive and alert, all qualities that pay well in the Fight Game. As the Germans encouraged boxing shows for entertainment during their occupation, van Dam was able to keep in fistic trim, even if his bouts were limited in number. Also, his participation in the sport covered up his underground activities and saved him from being sent to a labour camp or an even worse fate.

Van Dam was 25 when the war ended and he was able to renew his ring career. He was now champion of Holland and jogged along meeting the pick of continental middleweights in the principal cities of Europe. The first London saw of him was in January 1949 when he was engaged by Jack Solomons to meet Albert Finch at the Albert Hall. The Croydon man was fast moving towards a shot at the British title at that time and his admirers received a shock when he was well outpointed by the Flying Dutchman, who had him guessing with a full reportoire of fast punches. The fact that he also put Albert on the canvas stamped Lucien as a class boxer.

The following year he was back again to lose surprisingly to a lanky coloured gentleman named Bill Jackson and it was hereabouts that Susan took a hand. She could not and would not believe it, because Jackson was an 'unknown' in Holland, and not much more than that in England.

Her first move was to get a return contest with the coloured man and, if Lucien had any doubts about her fitness in a managerial capacity, they were utterly dispelled when he knocked out Jackson in a single round. That was something like revenge, and when he had beaten Fernando Jannilli, of Italy, successfully defended his Dutch title against Job Roos, and outpointed George Amato – four fine wins on the trot – she let it be known that she would not object to her man taking on the redoubtable Sugar Ray Robinson.

The sensational coloured American was making a barnstorming tour of Europe, and a Brussels promoter wanted to feature him at the Palais des Sports there. The van Dams did not want a second invitation. The fact that Lucien was getting £4,000 was more than gratifying. He thrilled the fans by putting up a remarkable resistance until late in the third round. Then Robbie swung a most doubtful punch to the body and the

Dutchman went crashing to the canvas in an agony of pain.

Everyone but Sugar Ray and the referee thought it was a foul blow and the way Lucien clutched his abdomen and writhed on the floor made it clear that the world champion's aim had been considerably adrift. Van Dam would never have beaten the count, but unfortunately the timekeeper intervened at 'nine', so they carried the poor Hollander back to his corner and revived him sufficiently to answer the bell for round four. He staggered out like an automaton, and Robinson had nothing more to do than hook him hard on the chin with his left fist. Down went van Dam, stretched out at full length, and he stayed there for the full ten seconds and a number of minutes as well.

Examining Lucien in the dressing-room, a doctor found the fighter had been badly fouled. 'A very low blow, indeed,' he told reporters. 'It could not have been lower.' Susan was disappointed, but not dismayed. She still thought her husband's place was at the top of the middleweight division. Robinson had no room in his timetable for a return contest, so what about Randolph Turpin?

The European middleweight title had fallen vacant, so she submitted Lucien's name as a logical contender. The European Boxing Union accepted the nomination and paired him with the British champion; Jack Solomons then secured the match and promised the winner a fight with Robinson for the world's crown. The van Dams knew that Turpin was a tough proposition, but neither of them was worried. 'You stand up and box him, darling,' said the sensible Susan. 'Do as you did when you fought Finch and we can have that big house we want with a room each for the kids.' (Only she said it in Dutch.) She accompanied her husband to Harringay Arena, sure in her heart that this would be the turning point in his career. She was dead right.

The big North London hall was packed and while the popular Dutchman was given a most cordial reception, the ovation to Turpin shook the walls. Van Dam was all smiles and confidence. Randy, the sides and back of his head closely shaven, looked at the peak of physical fitness. They were scheduled to travel fifteen (three-minute) rounds at 11st. 6lb, and at the weigh-in Turpin was three-quarters of a pound inside, the heavier man by twenty-eight ounces.

The French referee, M. Scheman, called them together in the centre of the ring for a few cautionary words and the fight for the vacant middleweight championship of Europe began. It was over in quicker time than it will take me to write about it – and I am no sluggard with a typewriter. As soon as they got into range, light lefts were exchanged and they circled the ring with the Dutchman going backwards and his opponent gliding after him, poised on his toes, eager to play havoc with this thundering fists.

Suddenly Randy became a furious bundle of action. He hit out swiftly with both hands, left and right swings landing on van Dam's protecting arms. They clinched and the calm Dutchman stepped back then shot a left to the head. A sizzling right from Randy whistled past Lucien's chin, the Dutch champ stabbed out another left, then found himself on the ropes. In went Turpin, hitting out lustily. Van Dam slipped away and turned, pushing out another left. Then Randolph banged in a vicious left hook that caught the Dutchman flush on the point of the chin.

It was the pay-off punch. Lucien's legs buckled under him and everyone knew he must go down. Before he had started to drop, however, over came a swift, chopping right that landed in the centre of the Dutchman's jaw and sent him skating to the canvas on his side. Any hopes of van Dam beating the count evaporated when he rolled over on to his back. The ten seconds were tolled off without Lucien moving a muscle. He remained unmoving while his seconds worked over him and Susan watched anxiously from a nearby aisle.

She put her hand to her mouth to stifle a scream as a doctor climbed into the ring; she clapped both hands over her ears to drown the prolonged roar that came from the jubilant fans at Turpin's amazing victory. They had seen only 48 seconds of fighting for their money, but they were happily satisfied. Susan fled. She ran to the dressing-room, there to await with heart-pounding apprehension, the return of her fighter – and husband.

In her heart she knew it was the last of the big-time so far as they were concerned, but she wanted the first suggestion of retirement to come from her husband – not herself. Physically, Lucien had not suffered from his lightning defeat at the hands of Turpin; a clean-cut k.o. is far less injurious than a prolonged and systematic battering into submission. A rest of seven weeks, and he was ready to resume his fighting career. At past thirty years of age he could not expect to regain his former prominence, yet he won seven bouts in succession over good-class opposition in Dutch rings before the year was out. He then accepted an offer to box in Paris. His opponent was Claude Milazzo, a French Tunisian, nine years his junior, who was too fast for the veteran, and van Dam was adjudged a points loser after ten enduring rounds. On the way home he came to the conclusion that it was time he gave up swapping punches. No one was more pleased than Susan when he told her of his decision. She realised that in her eagerness to see him gain world fame they had aimed too high.

21

Too Much Fighting Brought Divorce

Joe Louis

Before Joe Louis Barrow was seventeen, his mother bought him a violin. They were living in Detroit then and there was a national economic depression that had half-closed the Ford factory, putting her husband out of work. She knew a musician who was earning 35 dollars a week in a band. Joe, next youngest of her eight children, was kicking his heels with nothing to do, so she sent him to a music teacher at a dollar a lesson. She imagined that in a few weeks he would be an accomplished violinist.

Joe tucked the violin under his arm and trudged off. After six lessons he knew no more than when he started, except that he hated violin playing. Next time he was due for a lesson, he hid the instrument behind an ash can and spent the dollar on boxing instruction at the local boys' club. All the healthy kids in the neighbourhood, white or coloured, wanted to be boxers. As amateurs they could win food vouchers that were changeable at the grocers. And most families were short of food.

After his training session, Joe would pick up his violin and go home. One day he found his music teacher there and his mother asked him where he had been and what he had done with the lesson money. He blurted out that he had been spending the money at the gymnasium learning to be a boxer. He would rather be a fighter than anything else in the world.

'Well, son,' she said, 'I guess it is no use trying to force you to do something against your nature. But if you *are* going to be a boxer, Joe, make sure you're a good one.'

For his first amateur bout he weighed 12st. and was knocked down seven times and stopped in two rounds. Joe was a sore-looking object when he handed his mother a merchandise voucher for seven dollars. He felt he never wanted to box again. She encouraged him. 'You have got to stick at anything if you want to be good at it,' she told him. 'If you've got it in you to be a boxer, you will have learned a lot from tonight.'

The youngster made slow but steady progress. In two years he had 54 bouts, winning 43 inside the scheduled distance and 7 on decisions, with 4 losses. Apart from a strong physique and the ability to do what he was told, Joe had little else. He did not get the right sort of food, he boxed in a pair of old tennis shoes, he had to take his bandages off carefully so they could be used again and again. He went into the ring with a small towel round his dusky shoulders.

A local business man, John Roxborough, who followed amateur boxing, took an interest in Joe Barrow. He bought him an outfit so that he could go into and win the Golden Gloves tourney in Chicago. He shortened his name to Joe Louis. Later on, when the youngster wanted to turn professional, Roxborough invited him to stay in his home. Mrs Barrow made no objection, and for the first time Joe lived well. He was given some pocket money and spent almost every day in a gymnasium under the care of Jack Blackburn, a former highly-rated lightweight, who was employed as his trainer.

Joe had his first paid fight in July 1934 at the age of twenty. It was the main event at the Bacon Casino in Chicago and was broadcast. It lasted less than a round. His mother listened in. She listened in to every fight he had until her son bought her a new house in Detroit and installed a television set. Then she watched every fight of his until the time when he made a regretful comeback at the age of 36 and lost to Ezzard Charles in 1950. She never looked in at boxing after that.

Purses grew with every contest. His picture began to appear in the papers, he found himself a celebrity. Only 4 of his first 27 bouts went the distance. He earned such a reputation as a knockout specialist the fight scribes called him 'The Brown Bomber'. When he beat Charley Massera in three rounds, he returned the 270 dollars his mother had received when the family was on relief in the depression days. A week before his

21st birthday he beat Gene Stanton, also in three rounds, and the next day bought himself a Buick.

That was the last of his build-up fights. Roxborough had joined forces with Promoter Mike Jacobs, who was set on putting the Madison Square Garden Corp. out of business with his newly-formed 20th Century Sporting Club. By monopolising the services of Louis, Uncle Mike knew he could not miss.

Joe became world famous the night he destroyed Primo Carnera, former heavyweight champion of the world, in six rounds. He ruined the giant Italian as a fighter. The purse of 60,000 dollars ascribed to Louis was the biggest sum ever paid a boxer in his first year as a professional. It was only the start of total ring earnings amounting to over four millions.

One day a friend brought Marva Trotter to watch Joe working-out. She was a stenographer, an intelligent, well-educated girl who wasn't all that interested in boxing, but was certainly attracted to this beautifully built young athlete. They became firm friends. Joe didn't say much, but what he said was sincere. He was good company and danced well. They decided to get married.

Louis told Mr Roxborough, who asked how soon. 'Right after the Max Baer fight,' suggested Joe. 'Right *before*,' snapped his patron. 'I don't want a wedding on your mind when you are fighting that feller.' So, a few hours before taking the ring at the Yankee Stadium in New York, Joe and Marva were quietly wed in her apartment, with only a few relatives present.

To get there had been quite an adventure. News of the forthcoming marriage had spread throughout Harlem and Joe, who was staying at an hotel, could not get out because the landings, stairways, hall and porch were packed with cameramen, reporters and hundreds of onlookers. He had to come down from the fifth floor by the fire escape and take a taxi from a side street. He beat Baer in four rounds and when they got back to their new Chicago home ten thousand people stood in the street and cheered and they had to make many appearances at their bedroom window before the fans would disperse.

Marva's happiness was not lasting. Her husband was heading

straight for the world's heavyweight championship and his time was fully occupied by those around him, anxious to see that he did not take a wrong step towards that goal. He had already beaten two ex-champions, Carnera and Baer; now Uncle Mike planned a third, the tough and experienced Max Schmeling, from Germany.

If Louis had one fault in his boxing make-up it was a tendency to hold his left hand too low. His trainer had observed it and worked on Joe to correct it; Schmeling also had noticed the flaw and he worked on it to the Brown Bomber's downfall. Max let his weighty right hand go in the fourth and sent Louis flat on his back. It was the first time he had ever been put down as a professional and was dazed and bewildered. Yet he got up to beat the count and fought back instinctively until the twelfth round when Schmeling tagged him again. This time it was the real thing. Joe fell forward on to his face, buried his head in his arms as if he was sleeping and they could have counted a hundred.

When he got home Joe told Marva: 'I guess I lost, honey.' 'I know,' she answered. 'I was there.' Unbeknown to her husband she had gone to the fight with a girl friend and suffered agonies from the first knockdown to the last.

'Well,' remarked Blackburn, anxious to smooth things over. 'Nobody got killed and we can start all over again.' 'You're right nobody got killed, but no thanks to you or anyone else,' snapped Marva. 'Joe needs a break and I'm taking him away for a few weeks. Do you realise that we have been married for nine months and haven't had a honeymoon yet? '

They went away and had great fun, then the road back to the championship began. It took exactly a year, and Joe's supporters got the shock of their lives when Jimmy Braddock, the veteran champion, put him on the canvas in the first round with a right clip to the chin. But this was not a Schmeling wallop, and Joe got up to mechanically reduce his rival to impotence. By the eighth Braddock was exhausted and could take no more. He went down for the full count and the Brown Bomber had become heavyweight champion of the world.

Within ten weeks he had put his newly-won title at stake

against Tommy Farr and was given a strenuous time by the British champion before gaining a close points win. After that came Uncle Mike's 'Bum of the Month' parade, in which Louis defended the championship twenty times in five years against the best heavies that could be found.

Some were in the pushover class, but others were not, among them Max Schmeling, over whom Joe gained a one-round revenge win; Tony Galento, who put Louis down; Buddy Baer, who shoved the champ out of the ring; and Billy Conn, who was on the point of winning the decision when he got over-confident and paid the full penalty. Money was pouring in and Joe, with so many deserving relatives and a quickly acquired taste for a good time, spent it as fast as it came.

Marva had everything she wanted, but wasn't happy. She was tired of Joe being away in training so often and for such long spells. The money did not compensate for being a boxing widow. Jacqueline was born in 1943 and that brought them closer together for a spell, but it did not last. Joe went into the Army to box exhibitions and go on extensive tours throughout the United States and in Europe. He hardly ever saw his home.

For several years Marva had been urging her husband to retire from boxing. He had plenty of opportunities in other spheres of life, but Joe liked the Fight Game and the company of men who spoke his language. He just could not give it up. They were divorced in 1945 and in lieu of alimony Mrs Louis received a one-fourth manager's contract which entitled her to a sizable cut from every subsequent purse her husband received. She put the money into a trust fund for her daughter and kept herself by earning a startling salary as a cabaret singer.

After the war Louis had two more title defences, then he and Marva made it up and got married again. Again she tried hard to get him to retire. 'Do it now, Joe,' she pleaded. 'Before some youngster hits you too hard for your own good.' So Joe eased off boxing, and Marva gave him a son, Joe Junior. He took up bowling and golf and like the fanatic he was, he stayed away from home even more. An offer came for a daily training session at a fitness exhibition at Earl's Court, so Louis and his wife came to London and once again enjoyed life together. But once they were back in America the old routine started, and when Marva heard that her husband intended to make a comeback, she left him once more – this time for good.

Joe just had to come back. For one thing he had neglected to pay income tax over the years and now owed Uncle Sam a pile of dollars; for another, they had installed Ezzard Charles in his place as champion and he felt more than a trifle jealous. Finally, he still loved fighting. After a reign of over eleven years, and with the record number of 25 successful title defences to his credit, the undefeated world heavyweight champion came back – to defeat!

Charles outboxed him by a decisive margin. His mother switched off her TV set and Marva sobbed. The great Brown Bomber was no more, and to convince Joe of that fact, Rocky Marciano knocked him out a year later – just as his wife had predicted some youngster would.

22

Beautiful Secretary
Cost Him his Crown

Ingemar Johansson

It was a bright May morning in 1959 and the fight mob was assembled at the Swedish-American pierhead. Ingemar Johansson, next challenger for the world heavyweight title, was expected, and it was customary to pay respect to European contenders. There had not been many over the years and most of them not worth seeing off home again. But there had been Max Schmeling from Germany, and Primo Carnera from Italy, both of whom had won the big title, and the Welshman Tommy Farr, who came close to success. And you never know.

There were the newspaper boys and their cameramen, there was the reception committee headed by Bill Rosensohn, New York's mushroom promoter. There were some officials from the Boxing Commission, and one or two less authentic gentlemen, who were hopeful of being able to muscle in on the project. The liner came in and they went aboard. A press conference was arranged in one of the lounges. There was no difficulty in picking out the Swedish heavyweight, who looked smaller than expected. But who were the mixed assembly surrounding him?

'My friend and adviser, Eddie Ahlquist,' beamed Ingemar. 'My father, my mother, my sister Eva, my brother Rolf, his girl-friend Annette, my oldest brother Henry – and this is Birgit Lundgren, my secretary-fiancée.' Birgit was quite a dish, and she came in for almost as much attention as Johansson. What did she do? 'I attend to the mail, keep the newspaper clippings, make sure the engagements do not overlap, and am the social companion.' Papa was manager, Mamma was cook and housekeeper, brother Rolf was sparring-partner, while sister Eva and brother Henry were consultant members of the family.

This was something new. A fighter bringing the entire family and his girl friend. What is more, the whole bunch moved into Johansson's training camp. There had never been so much feminine influence surrounding a boxer preparing for a title bout or for any form of contest. It was so out of keeping with established procedure that the wise guys shook their heads. Floyd Patterson has had another pushover picked for him, they reckoned. This is a pretty boy who has fluked his way into a championship fight. How could it be more than a fiasco?

True, the Swede was unbeaten in 21 professional fights, but who had he beaten? He had won the Euopean title by knocking out Franco Cavicchi, a not-so-hot Italian, in 13 rounds; he had stopped three of the best British heavies, Peter Bates (2), Henry Cooper (5) and Joe Erskine (13) but they were hardly in the world class. The only performance of real significance was a sensational one-round win over Eddie Machen, a leading contender for the championship. But that could be explained away. The coloured boxer had not fought in five months and it was his first bout abroad. Maybe he had run into a sucker punch.

The Swede's training schedule was likewise eyebrow-raising, his methods being vastly different from the routine adopted by top-rated fighters. Ingemar ran six miles every morning through the Catskill Mountains, drank a vast quantity of milk, was 'kind' to his sparring partners in a prolonged session of light boxing, did a varied and most intricate series of calisthenics, and used a Swedish contraption, known as a 'slungboll', to quicken his reactions. This was a soft leather ball suspended at the end of an 18-inch strap handle. It moved with the speed and unpredictability of an opponent's bobbing and weaving head.

Although reported to possess a right-hand punch of knock-out power, Ingemar never showed it once during his public work-outs. The sceptics got to believe it did not exist. They were also astonished at the way he spent the rest of the day. He just lolled around, swimming, reading and sleeping. He seemed to be able to drop off to sleep at any time.

In the evenings he shocked the critics by going to a restaurant for a light meal and to dance with Birgit. He stayed to watch the cabaret show and went back to camp in the early hours of the morning. He caused the biggest sensation, however, by stopping all training five days before the date of the championship fight. It was an unheard-of practice and the gamblers immediately boosted the energetic and conscientious Patterson to a 4-1 favourite.

It meant, however, that the Swede entered the Yankee Stadium ring the most relaxed person in New York. Even the 24-hour delay brought about by rain did not perturb him, or the fact that among the multitude of fans only the members of his family were there to root for him.

For two rounds he let Patterson do all the attacking, being satisfied to paw away with a long left jab while making good use of the ring. Then, midway through the third, the champion dropped his guard the merest fraction of an inch and for the first time America saw Ingo's Bingo. That powerful right, which Johansson had kept out of sight and used only in secret training sessions, flashed out, crashed against Patterson's chin and his fighting wits were scattered. Seven times in that sensational round the champion hit the canvas. Six times he got up and was allowed to continue, but on the seventh occasion the referee put an end to the slaughter.

Johansson had become the first of his countrymen to win the world heavyweight title. As he climbed out of the ring, he kissed his big right hand for the photographers and in the dressing-room, with everyone crying with happiness, he kissed his father, his mother, his sister, his brother Rolf, his brother Henry, and Annette. He didn't kiss Birgit, though. He did not reckon to do that in public.

Patterson was entitled to a return contest, but no one was sure that he wanted it. He had suffered humiliating defeat and the fact that he had let down his race and the American boxing public left him wretched beyond belief. He had left the Stadium wearing dark glasses, now he hid himself away from everyone except his wife and child. But time heals all wounds, and after a long spell of self-condemnation and meditation, the news flashed that Floyd would meet Johansson in an effort to regain his lost crown. The fact that no one in ring history had ever won back the heavyweight title did not deter him.

Patterson's enemies said it was the fortune he would get as the loser that was the big inducement, but although the second fight was not due to take place until a year after the first, Floyd went off to an almost monastic training camp as soon as the contracts were signed to give himself an even more rigorous preparation then before. Not so Johansson. He was in great demand, both in Sweden and America, and set out to cash in on his title and enjoy himself to the full.

There was a film to be made in Hollywood, there were shows and social engagements to fill. Aided and abetted by the beautiful Birgit, he did not miss a trick, posing for advertising campaigns, opening functions, even writing a book. During the twelve months Ingemar shunned the gloves and kept clear of the gymnasium. He did his roadwork on the dance floor and restricted his exercising to playing tennis, golf and horse riding. Before leaving for America for the return Patterson bout, he and Miss Lundgren announced they would be getting married in the autumn. Not that they needed an excuse for being together and enjoying life. It just fitted in with the dining, dancing and night-clubbing.

When he and the family opened his training camp, no one came along expecting to see anything different from before. They didn't, in fact, it was even less like the real thing. Johansson shocked them by swimming in the lake with his fiancée as part of his Press work-out. He still lazed and loafed around, only this time it is doubtful if there was any secret training. As before, he did not throw his famous Bingo right for the benefit of the onlookers. They knew all about it now, as did Patterson, so there was really no need to waste energy in tossing it.

They made the Swede an 8-5 favourite and no one among the hundred-odd newspaper men tipped Floyd to win. Of the 31,892 fans who crowded into the New York Polo Grounds, none expected a different result from the first meeting. They came along just to see if Johansson could do it quicker this time and how many times the Hand of Thor would have to strike before Patterson was counted out.

After coasting through the first round, Ingemar let his faithful right hand loose midway in the second and the fans tensed themselves for the first knockdown. It never came. Patterson had pulled back slightly and taken the blow on his forehead. Even so, the sheer power behind the punch set him staggering, but failed to knock him off his feet.

Johansson threw another, but again was off the target as the ex-champion ducked and took the punch on the top of his head. But it was only a glancing blow and Floyd did not falter. Instead, he came back with a left hook that took the Swede by surprise. The champion was astounded. He had hit his rival just as hard – or had he? But it hadn't knocked the fight out of Floyd. Ingemar tried to nail him again throughout the remainder of the round. He tried all through the third and the fourth, then he began to have his doubts.

Patterson was as strong as ever, confident too. He came out for the fifth in hurricane style, stabbed the flat-footed Swede swiftly to the face, jumped inside to rattle away with a hearty tattoo of combination punches, then whipped over a right to the chin. It was a beauty, shaking Johansson down to his toes. Before he could get out of range, Floyd banged in a left hook to the jaw and behold – it was Ingo who was on the floor.

Now the fans had something to shout about. They saw the Swede groping on the canvas, blood trickling from his mouth, a gash showing over his left eye. He pulled himself up at 'nine'. Another left hook to the head sent Johansson reeling into the ropes. He tried to cover up, but Patterson was like a panther now and his swift blows thudded against the champion's head.

He was a doomed man, his face a mask of bewilderment. He could read the 'killer' look in the coloured man's eyes, and, like a rabbit attacked by a snake, stood there paralysed in brain and body. Patterson had only to land one last left hook. It smote Johansson full on the point of the chin and sent him crashing on his back, his head striking the boards with a bang.

He was completely unconscious and the count was a mere formality. Ingemar remained 'out' for eight minutes and it was another ten before he was able to leave the ring. Time of the round, 1min. 51sec. Birgit had seen it all, but could not believe it. Neither could her fiancé. They left the Polo Grounds in a daze, and had to wait for the newspapers to find out exactly how catastrophe had overtaken them.

Had they learned a lesson? It seemed unlikely, when Floyd and Ingemar had their rubber meeting in the Convention Hall at Miami Beach nine months later. While Patterson underwent a strenuous preparation in almost complete privacy at Spring Valley near New York, Johansson preferred to train among the lush surroundings of the Seebreeze Motel at Palm Beach. Here he again took things easy, spending far too much time on the beach with Birgit and not enough on the road or in the gymnasium with his spar-mates. As before, the whole family were there with his mother supervising the cooking.

They were all at the ringside, eager to see Ingo win back his title and he brought them to the pitch of excitement in the very first round when he stabbed the agile Patterson back on his heels with a telling left and then flashed over his big right to send the champion flat on his back. For some unknown reason the referee went on counting to 'eight', although Floyd was on his feet almost immediately. But he had been badly shaken and the fans roared as another mighty right collided with the champion's chin and bowled him over again. Once more he was up on the sixth second, but still Referee Bill Regan went on counting to 'eight' and wasted more seconds – precious to Johansson – while he wiped Patterson's gloves before ordering the men to 'box-on'.

Ingo might have won in that sensational opening round but for those unnecessary mandatory counts; he needed to win early in the fight if he was to win at all. You need bags of stamina in the ring and his languid mode of training was not productive of that essential quality. By the sixth round Johansson was a spent force and a left hook to the chin from the now-revitalised Floyd had him in trouble. Before he could recover, a right hook caught him on his drooping jaw, followed by a clubbing right to the head that had him blundering to the canvas; although he struggled to his feet, he just failed to beat the count.

There wasn't a lot after that, just four contests in the next two years; although he won all of them, the opposition was not of the highest class, and it came as no real surprise when he announced his retirement from the ring at the age of thirty to get married to Birgit and take up a number of business interests.

23

Wife and Six Children Made Him Champ

Jersey Joe Walcott

Jersey Joe Walcott got out of the car, said goodnight to his friends and went into his home. They had wanted to stay out for a while, to have a meal and talk over the night's events. They would have followed him in but he did not invite them. The old boxer was sick of the Fight Game. He threw his kit into the cupboard under the stairs and entered the living-room. The whole family was up waiting for him, the whole seven of them.

There was his wife Lydia, his eldest son Arnold, the three girls Doris, Ruth and Alva, the baby Edna and his youngest boy Vincent. They were all looking glum. Ruth wanted to know why he had not been given the decision. Arnold suggested that he had been robbed. His wife was more anxious to know if he had been hurt and what had happened. Then Vincent exploded: 'Where's the turtle?' he demanded. 'You said you would bring home the turtle. I've been looking forward to playing with it.'

'They let Louis keep the turtle,' answered his father quietly. 'The referee thought I had won it, so did the eighteen thousand fans. But the two judges voted for Joe, so I guess he is still the champion.' He patted his disappointed son on the head and told him how sorry he was not to have kept his word, but the Boxing Commission had promised that he should have a return fight with Louis in six months' time.

Lydia sighed. She had been married to this fighting man for fourteen years. In that time he had not enjoyed a single break until it was too late. Fancy keeping a man waiting until he was nearly 33 before giving him a championship chance. Anyway, there he was, disappointed, but with no bones broken. He had earned nearly 30,000 dollars to meet the champion and his share of that sum should keep them comfortable meanwhile.

She and her children had watched the New York fight on television. The first time ever a heavyweight championship fight had been shown by this medium in America. She had seen her husband put Louis down for a count and, in her opinion, outbox the champion in the majority of the rounds. Ruby Goldstein had scored the fight for her Joe, but the two judges had gone the other way. Even Louis thought he had lost, because he was on his way out of the ring believing himself to be an ex-champion when they called him back to raise his hand as the winner.

Walcott secured the second match with the Brown Bomber according to schedule. But this time he did not lose by a disputed decision, Louis saw to that. He trapped old Jersey Joe into making a false move in the eleventh round and knocked him out with a left hook to the chin. There were no complaints from the family, even Vincent made no mention of the 'turtle'. They were all so silent that the father put his boxing kit back under the stairs. He looked sorrowfully at the worn boots, the buckled protector and the blood-stained trunks, then shut the door on them.

He had been eighteen years in the Fight Game – on and off. Had been chiselled by every conniving manager in the business, and only a small percentage of his meagre earnings had found their way into his own pocket. Somehow 'de ducks' had the better of him. They would tell him he was due to get so many dollars. It had sounded wonderful, even with the managerial cut of fifty percent. Then 'de ducks' had spoilt it. 'We deducts a hundred bucks for publicity, then we deducts the wages of the sparmates. We also deducts our expenses, taxi fares, telephone calls, entertaining the Press boys, etcetera.' Then Uncle Sam got into the deducting racket, and by the time Jersey Joe received what was left, he had to go out and get a job to pay the rent.

He must have quit the boxing business a dozen times. He worked as a labourer on the docks and that kept the ever-growing family from sheer want, if not in comfort. Then someone would come along and proposition him back into the ring. Lydia would sigh, wash out the trunks, the bandages and the dressing-robe and resign herself to the inevitable. Joe might win, he might lose. If he won the managers of other heavyweights blacklisted him; if he lost, promoters were anxious to forget him.

Round about the New Year of 1945, when Walcott was close to his 31st birthday, he had steady employment at a soup factory in Camden, New Jersey. The fight kit had been stowed away out of sight and his ring days were in his past life. In the town was a keen operator named Felix Bocchichio (he told me you pronounced it 'Bocheecheo'). He had a few dollars lying dormant and a big liking for boxing. He sought out Vic Marsillo who had a lease on the only fight arena in Camden and asked why he did not use it.

Mr Marsillo agreed there were plenty of fight followers in the neighbourhood, but that the fans preferred going over into New York. If there was some local talent, he might be able to attract them, but there wasn't any, so what was the use? Felix reminded him there was an old heavyweight living in the town who according to the record book had not fought in the place of his birth for the last seven years. Bluntly he was informed that the reason was because Walcott would not draw a house full of free tickets.

Bocchichio was not convinced. He called on Jersey Joe that evening and found him helping Lydia with the washing-up – no light task in their home. The old fighter listened. Then he indicated his six children and their mother and said he was happy to leave things as they were, that with his wages he could just about pay for their food and clothing. He did not fancy being beaten up by a youngster for a few extra dollars.

Felix urged that he had enough talent to beat any of the young heavies of the day; that Joe Louis had run out of challengers and after years in the U.S. Army was nowhere near so formidable as in the past. He told Walcott he would guarantee him six bouts in Camden from which he would earn some real money for a change. Next day he sent round a large box of groceries and a cheque for five hundred dollars. Jersey Joe looked at Lydia, she shrugged her shoulders, routed out his fighting gear once again, folded it up neatly and pushed the lot into a bag.

They felt sorry for the old man when he trudged into the gymnasium and started to change. He had not engaged in a serious contest for five years and now all he was fit for was being a chopping-block for some up-and-coming kid. But the veteran won in two rounds, then went on fighting with such success that the fans crammed in to see him, and he became a local hero. The Walcott family's standard of living began to rise and his name got into the headlines, especially after he whipped big Joe Baksi, whom many thought would be the next world champion. Lydia would not go to see him fight, nor did she listen-in or watch him on television. But the kids did, and they went crazy when they knew that Pop was going to fight for the title. Unfortunately Vincent got the wrong impression.

They wanted to put Joe Louis into Madison Square Garden in a ten-round exhibition match for a charity show, and they picked on Jersey Joe as his sparmate, reckoning that the old-timer was safe to stay the distance with the Brown Bomber. But the fans were not interested, and the tickets remained unsold. 'All right,' grunted Promoter Mike Jacobs. 'they can have a championship fight for the same money.' So Walcott's big chance came when he least expected it.

That was where you came in, and now Jersey Joe had been given two opportunities to win the big crown and his kit was back in the cupboard under the stairs. But not for long. Within a few months Louis announced his retirement and they selected Ezzard Charles, the 'Cincinnati Flash', to fight for the vacant title. His opponent – Jersey Joe Walcott. They met in Chicago.

Charles was seven years his junior, and it was generally regarded as a gift for the younger man. The old warrior had not fought for a year, so it was not surprising that he lost on points. But the contest had been close enough to warrant a return bout, which was staged in Detroit, and this time Jersey Joe had the satisfaction of putting the new champion on the canvas. But he could not keep him there and once again Walcott was declared a points loser. Four months later they had a third match, mainly because there was no one else capable of giving Charles a worthwhile fight. But they took the precaution of putting it on at Pittsburgh.

The experts thought Walcott was in for another beating, but Joe was not bothered. So far he had been involved in four lucrative title fights, now he was to have a fifth. Win or lose, it was all good money, and he thought he knew enough about Charles to beat him this time. Accordingly he set off with such vigour that the younger man was taken completely by surprise. Jersey Joe belted into him with speed and fury. The fans wondered where he had found the energy. Then, in the seventh round, he seized a split-second opening, banged in a perfect left hook, and the champion went down in a heap for the full count.

No one could believe it. Old Jersey Joe champion at last? It had taken him 21 years to get there. At $37\frac{1}{2}$ he was the oldest fighter ever to win the big title. There was a big wide grin on his face as he climbed out of the ring. He had reached his goal after giving up the idea a dozen times. He had beaten disappointment and frustration, he had conquered chicanery, he had routed the racketeers. Thanks to a clean life and a belief in physical fitness, he had achieved the impossible and gained the ring's greatest prize with all the odds loaded heavily against him. By sheer courage and opportunism he had at last done something to earn the love and respect of his wife and family.

When he woke up in his hotel room next morning, he climbed out of bed and looked in the mirror. 'Morning, champ,' he said, then picked up the phone: 'Send someone down to a pet store,' he told the desk clerk. 'I want the best-looking turtle they've got, one with plenty of life in him, because he's going to need it. Have him packed in a box ready for me when I check out.'

So far, his tough old fists had won him over half a million dollars, and there was another half-million to come, on a fourth match with Ezzard Charles, after he had enjoyed the fruits of being world champion for a year. This he won on points; then came a defence against Rocky Marciano, a young, strong and vigorous challenger, so far unbeaten in his professional career.

They paid him 138,000 dollars to face the 'Brockton Blockbuster' in Philadelphia, plus another 140,000 dollars, his share of the film receipts. And no one gave him a chance. Yet, Jersey Joe gave the fans the thrill of a lifetime when he dropped the unbeaten Marciano in the first round with a powerful clip to the chin.

Only a rock-like Rocky could have got up from that punch; no other man in the world would have survived it. But Marciano stood straight up without taking a count and then bulldozed poor old Jersey Joe about, finally battering him down to defeat in round thirteen.

Walcott was entitled to a return fight according to the contract. He talked it over with Lydia. She said 'No.' 'I'm guaranteed a quarter-million bucks, honey,' he argued. 'That's too much money to shrug your shoulders at.' She gave in. 'Okay, Joe,' she said. 'But remember, you're forty years old next birthday. And remember something else, I love you. So make it short.'

It was Marciano who made it short, but not the way she imagined. Rocky finished the gallant ex-champion in precisely 2min. 25sec. Joe and the kids were disappointed, but his wife was happy. 'I could kiss that Rocky,' she said when her husband got home. 'Think of all the punches you didn't have to take.'

Today, Jersey Joe is attached to the New Jersey Police Department as a special investigator to combat juvenile deliquency. They regard him as an inspiration to the youth of America.

24

Singing Star
Wife Became No. 1 Fan

Sugar Ray Robinson

The important women in the fabulous life of Sugar Ray Robinson were those with the closest family ties. His mother, his two sisters, his loyal wife. Without their strong influence he might not have become one of the greatest fighters ever to pull on a pair of gloves. Perhaps the reason for this was the fact that when he had reached the age of twelve his parents parted company in Detroit and his mother, Mrs Walker Smith, took her family to New York and settled in West 114th Street. Before Evelyn (16) and Marie (15) got jobs for themselves, Ma secured work as a seamstress in a laundry. Junior was supposed to busy himself by going to school, but he spent more time in the streets than he did in the classroom.

You can learn a lot running wild in a teeming city. Young Walker Smith was a skinny, underweight kid, with plenty of devil, a lot of cheek, and a glib tongue. This got him into plenty of trouble and he had to fight or run to get out of it. If the opposition was too big to be handled with his fists he fled home. More than once, either Marie had to fight his battles for him, or Ma had to shoo off an irate pursuer.

As has happened many times, a priest intervened in a street scrap one day, taking both boys to the Salem Crescent Athletic Club run by an ex-boxer named George Gainsford. He liked the look of Walker Smith and found him a ready pupil. When the boy got home, he asked his mother for the money to pay his subscription. Somehow she scraped it up, and when she told me this story she added that it was the best investment she ever made. Gainsford was a big man: the boys called him 'Emperor Jones'. His influence over Smith was enough to take him off the streets and get him into the gymnasium for most nights of the week.

When Smith was 17, Gainsford gave him his first amateur bout, in a small club at Kingston, 90 miles out of New York. He wasn't really ready for contests, but the show was short of a bantamweight, the kid was eager, so George let him go on. 'You'll need an Amateur Athletic Union card to get by the officials,' the trainer told him. 'I'm giving you the one belonging to the boy who can't box tonight. Now don't forget – you are Ray Robinson when they call out the names.'

He has been Ray Robinson ever since. After he had won the Golden Gloves as a featherweight and turned professional, someone mentioned to Gainsford that he had found a very sweet fighter. 'Sure,' answered George. 'He's as sweet as sugar.'

His first paid bout was at Madison Square Garden against Joe Echeverria. His mother and sister Marie came to see him win in two rounds and after his bout he stayed on to watch the main event. It was a world welterweight title fight between Henry Armstrong and Fritzie Zivic. When the championship changed hands, Sugar Ray sat there and wept.

Armstrong had been his boyhood hero. He had vowed he would try and emulate Henry's great feat of being the holder of three world championships at one and the same time. Zivic treated the ageing 'Hurricane' in cruel fashion and when he got home Ray told the family that his one ambition was to give Zivic the hiding of his life.

'You could beat Zivic now,' encouraged Marie, but Ma had more sense. 'You will take him when Mr Gainsford says so,' she said. 'You're only a boy yet, and Fritzie is a grown man. Don't be impatient and don't stop training.' Sugar Ray remembered his mother's advice for 40 fights, all of which he won, 29 inside the distance. Then he took a bout in Detroit against a tough Bronx boy named Jake LaMotta, whom he had out-pointed in New York four months earlier without a great deal of trouble. Foolishly thinking that what he had done once he could do again, he shirked his training.

Halfway through this gruelling ten-rounder he went tired. In the eighth LaMotta knocked him through the ropes and at the end of the contest Robinson had been beaten for the first time. 'Let that be a lesson to you,' admonished Ma. 'You were getting too big for your boots and started loafing. You cannot be anything or get anywhere if you don't work for it. Boxing is a business, not something to play at.' He took that to heart. The advice lasted eight years and up to his next defeat, the time when Randy Turpin took away his middleweight title in London.

He licked LaMotta four times after that beating in Detroit, but could never erase the memory of that first setback. He moved into the big money, and when he won the vacant welter title by beating Tommy Bell, he bought a house for his mother in New York's West Bronx, paying 8,500 dollars for it and 3,000 dollars in furnishings. The first thing she did was to hang up twenty-three pictures of her famous son.

Just about this time another woman came into his life. She was Edna Mae Holly, a dancer in a night club, slender, glamorous, standing 5ft $2\frac{1}{4}$in. in high heels, with a figure that made men give a double-take. She was displaying this on the edge of a swimming pool one afternoon when Sugar came along, gave her a shove and sent her in the deep end. He had to marry her after that. She gave up dancing, not because she wished it, but because Sugar Ray laid down the law. 'No wife of mine is going to travel in one direction and me in another,' he told her. 'Then I'll be your No. 1 fight fan,' she declared.

The money rolled in. He successfully defended his welter title five times and then cast covetous eyes towards the middleweight throne. His old enemy Jake LaMotta was champion and the fight scene was shifted to Chicago. Already they had boxed 42 rounds with the score 3 to 1 in Robinson's favour. The fans expected that Jake would fight to the death in order to keep the championship.

Edna Mae had a ringside seat. Right from the starting bell she yelled at her husband to beat the living daylight out of LaMotta. Ray did not want any encouragement. He fought with an ice-packed brain, rigidly intent on winning another title. Jake put up grim resistance and by the 11th round, when he knew he was trailing on points, gave everything he had got to try and beat down this dancing phantom that kept catching him with punches that were slowly sapping his stamina.

He rushed the lighter man into the ropes. He caught the challenger with a vicious right to the body that made Sugar Ray fold up. He piled on the punches, he swarmed, he pounded. Mrs Robinson buried her face in her hands. She couldn't bear to see her husband's slim, elegant body being punched to pulp. Then a roar from the crowd had her wide-eyed and yelling again.

Robby had turned the champion round. He was giving back as good as he had received – more. He extinguished Jake's fire with a concentrated assault that drilled into the champion and reduced him to impotency. Midway through the 13th, with LaMotta rolling on the ropes, dazed, helpless, incapable of defending himself, the referee called a halt and Sugar Ray had gained his second world crown.

By now the Robinsons were in big business. In Harlem they had a cafe, a barber saloon, a dry-cleaning store, a lingerie shop and a block of flats. He was also licensed to lend money – up to 300 dollars. They decided to tour Europe. Ray had already enjoyed a month there, winning five bouts in an aggregate of thirty rounds, which more than paid expenses. Why not again?

With him went his customary entourage. There was Edna Mae and sister Evelyn. There was Mr and Mrs Gainsford. Also included were: Harry Wiley, his trainer, Pee Wee Beale, another trainer, Algar Clark, his secretary, Shelton Oliver, his golf partner, Roger Sim, his barber and Jimmy Karoubi, his dwarf mascot. Ma declined to join the circus – she was a bad traveller – but they took Ray's fuchsia-coloured Cadillac.

Sugar fought in Paris, Zurich, Antwerp, Liege, Berlin and Turin, all in the space of forty-one days. It was a triumphant tour that gave Jack Solomons a brainwave. With a lot of verbal persuasion and £26,000 financial inducement, he managed to get Robinson to defend his world middleweight title against Randy Turpin in London.

Who was Turpin, anyway? Champion of England! But that didn't mean much in American eyes. Champion of Europe!

Well, that didn't amount to much more. Said Edna Mae, encouragingly: 'They don't come any tougher than LaMotta, honey, and you finished him as a fighter. This English kid is due for a massacre.'

She went a bit further in the publicity line when I interviewed her a few days before the fight. 'You don't know Sugar,' she told me. 'He can dissect fighters as he boxes them. He will take this Turpin apart and let you see how he works. My man is the greatest.'

So along with 18,000 others, I went to Earls Court one July evening in 1951, occupying a Press seat. Behind me Edna Mae and Evelyn sat in the front row. They yelled for Sugar in unison. At first it was: 'Now take your time, honey. Beat him up slow but sure. Give him the cute treatment, Sugar, cut him down to size. Don't hurt him too hard, baby.'

That was from round one to ten, then the tempo and tune changed as Robinson emerged from a rally with a jagged gash over his left eye. Now it was: 'Be careful, honey. Move around Ray. Don't take any chances, man.' Turpin won handsomely on points after fifteen rounds I shall never forget. It was a victory that thrilled every fight fan in the United Kingdom, the greatest British ring triumph of the century.

Those who imagined that Ray Robinson was finished as a star fighter had to re-adjust their ideas. Sixty-four days later in New York, Sugar Ray got his title back, and full revenge, by stopping Turpin in ten rounds; he was to go on and make further ring history.

He made two more successful title defences, then challenged Joey Maxim for the light-heavyweight crown. To win three world titles was his peak ambition, but the gods were not with him that night. Putting up the greatest performance of his life, he outboxed the champion and must have won. But there happened to be a heat wave and, as much from his own exertions in an impossible atmosphere as anything that Maxim could contribute, Robinson collapsed in his corner at the end of the 13th and could not continue.

He announced his retirement from boxing and took up a dancing cabaret act, but the yen for the Fight Game was too strong. Two-and-a-half years later, this amazing man made the greatest comeback of all time. He needed to return to the ring, for while he had been in show business and travelling to all parts of America, the person engaged to look after his business affairs had proved inadequate to the task. He had not only landed Robinson in debt, but also had neglected to pay his income tax demands. Sugar Ray was coming up to his 35th year. He had kept himself fit with his dancing routines, but was nothing near the peak of his fighting days. He could earn 25,000 dollars a year in cabaret, but knew he could acquire more than that in a single contest once he got back into the big time. He told Edna Mae that he was planning a comeback and although she tried her hardest to talk him out of the idea, she gave him her fullest support once she realised that he was determined to do it.

He took the precaution of trying himself out in an exhibition contest in Canada, then went into a ten-round bout with Joe Rindone in Detroit, winning in the sixth round. Next he went to Chicago for another ten-rounder, this time against Ralph (Tiger) Jones. This one not only went the scheduled distance, but at the finish the ring-rusty Robinson found himself the loser on points. It looked like the end of the the comeback and on the way home to New York, both Gainsford and Wiley advised him to give up the attempt, in fact, they would not work with him again 'for his own good'. If they thought this would put paid to his return to boxing they were rudely mistaken. He would manage his own affairs and train himself.

He secured a match with Johnny Lombardo at Cincinnati and won on points after a struggle. Then he won a quick victory over Ted Olla in Milwaukee and a few days later Gainsford and Wiley called round to offer their help, but Robby refused to speak to them. They had deserted him when they thought the ship was sinking, now he had proved that he could do without them. Edna Mae was not so sure. She pointed out that while it was all right for him to be on his own for minor bouts, once he got back into championship class he would need them in his corner. They had looked after him from the beginning, were used to him and knew his individual requirements. What is more, he would not be allowed into a ring without seconds, no boxing commission would permit it. He would have to have someone and it might just as well be those he was used to.

So Robinson listened to his wife and Gainsford and Wiley returned to the fold. But the former atmosphere of comradeship had evaporated and deep down Sugar Ray knew that he was really on his own – that if the comeback was to prove successful it would be as a result of his own unaided efforts. It required the utmost faith in himself, strenuous work in the training camp and a dedicated approach to what seemed to most people to be a forlorn hope.

Edna Mae came to watch the work-outs and after one session she told him she thought he was trying too hard; that he was so anxious to regain his place in the boxing scene that he was forgetting all the tricks of the ring that had made success so easy in the past. 'You are boxing as though you are trying to make the grade, whereas you should be banking on your vast experience and winning on sheer know-how.'

It was sound advice. Robinson relaxed and from that moment the great comeback was an assured success. In four fights he had regained the middleweight title he had never lost by knocking out Carl (Bobo) Olson in two rounds, and in the next six years there were ten more lucrative championship matches. He set up a record by winning the world middleweight title five times. When he finally lost his crown to Paul Pender in Boston and failed to regain it in a return contest, Sugar Ray was all for continuing his ring career, but his wife had had enough. By that time he was forty. Anxious that he should not slip any further down the fistic scale, she urged him to find some other means of earning a living. But Sugar Ray thought he could carry on for a few more years and so there came a mutual parting of the ways.

25

Ma's Bread-Pudding was a Winner

Henry Cooper

Possibly the last thing a mother imagines is that any son she may bring into the world may one day become a professional boxer, and a champion at that. Mrs Lily Cooper, who married a man who liked boxing and was competent at it, and whose parents had both been useful with their fists, did not give the matter a thought when she produced twin boys in May 1934. Her sole concern was to bring them up as strong and healthy children to the utmost limit of her powers, and that meant plenty of good wholesome food, plus every encouragement to develop their bodies with athletic and sporting pursuits.

Henry was born twenty minutes ahead of George and they were as alike as if one was the mirrored reflection of the other. The nurse who placed them in their mother's arms cheerfully prophesied that they would grow into six-footers and undoubtedly liking the idea, Mrs Cooper did her best to see that they reached this eminence – at least she was determined that if they did not, it would be no fault of hers.

She did not have the easiest of tasks. War came when they were five years old, and she did not see her husband for the best part of four years. Already she had a nine-year old son, Bernard, so there were four mouths to feed on the scant allowance received by the wives of servicemen; rationing did not allow her to give them as much food as she would have wished. Very often her own plate received the smallest portion of what was available, and when the boys were at school she went out to work in order to supplement the meagre family budget.

The twins grew into high-spirited boys with a lust for

escapades and games. When their father returned from Burma he must have been delighted to find two eager lads ready and willing to be taught the rudiments of the Noble Art. There is a story that when they were sparring together, George put Henry down with a right-hander, the back of his head striking the kitchen stove, which knocked him out. Henry always maintained that he slipped in avoiding the punch, but true or not, Mum put an end to boxing in the house. They then performed with other boys on a patch of grass outside, wearing socks over their knuckles in place of the gloves they could not afford to buy.

When Mrs Cooper realised they were intent on becoming boxers, she was even more determined to build them up to full bodily development. She firmly believed that growing boys needed bulk and the best and cheapest means at her disposal was bread-pudding. She stuffed them with it and they loved it. Henry never forgot the recipe and always declared that it was 'lovely'. It must have been, because at his peak he stood 6ft 2in., and weighed $13\frac{1}{2}$ stones (189 pounds) while George (who boxed as 'Jim' because there was another heavyweight of the same name as himself) was of identical height, but scaled slightly more.

The brakes had to be put on the bread-pudding when they joined an amateur boxing club and progressed to the stage when they could engage in bouts: each of them lost his first four contests, mainly because they had come straight from home and a filling meal. 'You can't box on an empty stomach', Mum had declared, carving each a healthy portion of her speciality. But neither could they after she had stuffed them out to bursting point. So there was no bread-pudding on fight nights thereafter, although it continued to figure largely on the Cooper menu.

As the boys fought their way through the amateurs and competed for A.B.A. championships, their mother saw to their home care and sustenance. Henry was twice amateur light-heavyweight champion and represented his country in the Helsinki Olympic Games of 1952, being deprived of a medal by a bulky Russian, and then there was talk of them turning professional. Food rationing had come to an end and Ma was able to give them the tender steaks and fresh vegetables that a fighting man needs. She discovered the ideal diet essential to bringing a boxer to peak fitness and the energy for the fast pace at which modern boxing is fought. And if her bread-pudding was no longer a requirement, she knew that it had played a great part in building her boys into young giants.

After their National Service, they learned the plastering trade and soon proved adept at it, Henry left-handed and George right. It is strange that Henry was left-handed in everything he did except when it came to a boxing stance. Then he stood left-foot-forward, and not the reverse as do the 'southpaws' or left-handers. But whereas most 'orthodox' boxers carry their heaviest punch in their right hands, as did George, Henry's best delivery was his left hook which brought him fame and made history as 'Enery's 'Ammer. When it was obvious that a pro career lay ahead of them, they were lucky to have been in the plastering business because knocking up the mixture and applying it was muscle-building work for the hands, arms and shoulders, while it was a profitable craft to which they could return at any time they wished.

Mrs Cooper was not keen on them making a career of fist fighting, as naturally she was fearful that they might suffer mental or physical injury. Also, it took her mind back to the mid-30s when Raymond Bousquet, a French-Canadian middleweight who boxed under the name of Del Fontaine, fought too many contests in England, being reduced eventually from a strong and aggressive fighter to an animated punching-bag, finally being hanged for murdering his girl friend. When Ma was assured that under the rules and regulations of the British Boxing Board of Control her sons would be taking no such risk, her fears were alleviated, while the promise that in no circumstances would they ever fight one another brushed aside all her doubts and she proceeded to give them both all the encouragement and help they needed to get to the top.

Her aid was badly needed at times. Both Henry and George suffered the fighter's biggest bogey – cuts, a misfortune that brought short George's pro record, he being more prone to lacerations around the eyes than his brother. Henry managed to live with the problem, but suffered eye damage in the two most important contests of his life, the meetings with Cassius Clay – Muhammad Ali as later he called himself. The really desperate period in the Cooper family came in 1957 when the twins were 23 and they were both at the make-or-break stage in their fighting careers.

In September 1956 Henry had gone to Manchester, and, after putting down Peter Bates for a count of 'nine' in round one and, outpointing him steadily in every round thereafter, unluckily incurred an eye injury midway through the 15th and last round. He had the mortification of having the bout stopped and himself declared the loser on the referee's intervention. That started the rot. Being temporarily out of the hunt for the British heavyweight title, Henry challenged Joe Bygraves of Jamaica for his Empire crown, but was put down and out by a body blow in round nine. Three months later the twins journeyed to Stockholm, where George was disqualified for an alleged foul against Albert Finch in the seventh round, while Henry was knocked out in five rounds by Ingemar Johansson in a vain attempt to win the European championship.

Worse was to follow. Making a first bid for the British title and Lonsdale Belt at Harringay Arena, Henry was outpointed over fifteen rounds by Joe Erskine; on the same night George was halted in four rounds by Manuel Burgo because of a nasty eye wound, his third loss in four contests because of cuts. So far the Cooper professional record did not look at all convincing. Henry had now lost four bouts in succession, George five. Naturally they were dispirited; the thought of giving up boxing for good must have come into their minds more than once at this time. Pa Cooper shared their depression, but Ma kept quiet and did not attempt to influence them one way or the other, beyond saying that everyone suffered a bad patch at some time or the other.

The Cooper stock had hit rock bottom in England, no one was more aware of this than Manager Jim Wicks. He did not need to go the rounds of the promoters' offices to know that there was no work for them. Craftily he took Henry to Dortmund, where he outpointed Hans Kalbfell and made such an impression on the German fans that he was invited back to meet Heinz Neuhaus, against whom he was awarded a 'draw', which British boxers always regard as a points victory when fighting on the Continent. A third visit to Germany proved infuriating. At Frankfurt, Henry was paired with Erich Schoeppner whom he knocked cold in the sixth round with a solid left hook to the ear, only to find himself disqualified for alleged use of the 'rabbit' punch, which is a universal foul. In addition the authorities deducted half of the Englishman's purse of £1,400, whereupon the Cooper clan washed their hands of Germany and never fought there again.

It was the turning point in Henry's fortunes, however. He got off the canvas to stop Dick Richardson in five rounds at Porthcawl, then outpointed the highly-rated American, Zora Folley, at Wembley. He was now back in top-class boxing and achieved his great ambition by classically outpointing burly Brian London to win the British and Empire heavyweight titles. At last the Coopers had a champion in their midst and Ma could be proud of the eldest of her twin sons, and thankful that, despite all the difficulties, she had been able to rear a heavyweight who had proved himself the best in the country. She had had no part in teaching him the Noble Art, but she had supplied the power behind the punch, due no doubt to the plentiful supply of bread-pudding during his formative years.

It was, of course, the start of an amazing run of successes and setbacks, publicity, prosperity and popularity that was to continue for another twelve years, including the unsurpassed feat of winning outright three Lonsdale Belts, three times becoming European champion, and a magnificent attempt to win the world championship from one of the greatest holders of the richest prize in sport. It was a lengthy period in the public eye that was to make the name of Cooper a household word.

Ma surrendered most of her influence in January 1960 when Henry married Albina. He had met her when she was a waitress in a Soho restaurant where he ate fairly regularly following his morning training session at the Thomas a' Beckett gymnasium in the Old Kent Road. He had defended his Empire title successfully against Gawie de Klerk of South Africa at Porthcawl with a five-round win, and both his crowns against Joe Erskine, who was stopped in twelve rounds. Then he took a ten months' honeymoon in Italy during which his wife's parents and relatives were visited at Boccacci near Parma at the foot of the Appennines.

They set up home in Wembley, and Albina soon realised that being married to a fighting man was something special. She had to get used to his profession taking precedence over everything else in their family life; that the majority of his friends were connected with the sport in one way or another; that he needed special consideration and concessions in everything they did. What is more, she had to get used to the idea that before every contest he would be away from home for as long as five weeks; even when he had no fight in view, he would be putting in training sessions three or more times a week. She did not want to see him box; she kept away from the gymnasium and the training camp and took no part in any boxing discussions in their home, but at the same time she had to display an intelligent interest in all that was going on.

What she had to hide was her inborn fear that her husband would come to physical harm in his hazardous profession. She knew he took risks every time he climbed into a ring and was unable to relax until he was safely home again. Yet she had to send him off in the belief that she was unworried and fully convinced that he would return successful. Naturally, she preferred him to be victorious, but winning or losing was not important. What mattered most was that he should return unhurt.

Albina could share her husband's happiness and satisfaction in the hour of triumph, but had to be equal to the occasion in time of defeat. Fortunately for her the majority of Henry's fights during their married life were wins. In 27 bouts, 13 of which involved championships, he won all but seven. Of these setbacks, he lost two by the knockout route, being beaten by Zora Folley in two rounds in a return match, and by former world champion, Floyd Patterson, who knocked him out in four. There were the two bouts with Muhammad Ali (Cassius

Clay) that ended with the referee's intervention because of cut eyes, and three points losses against Roger Rischer, Amos Johnson and Joe Bugner.

The whole boxing world was agog when Henry made his bid for the world crown. He had given the champion such a tremendous battle when they first met, being one of the few to put 'The Greatest' on the canvas for a count and being unlucky that the American received a prolonged interval in which to recover from the knockdown. The whole fistic fraternity was anxious to see if Cooper could do it again when they met in the Arsenal Football Club's Stadium at Highbury in London on 21 May 1966: the vast arena was packed with fans eager to witness a British victory.

It was the one and only time Albina saw her husband fight. She had not wanted to go, but he persuaded her to attend, pointing out that in all probability there would never be another occasion like it. But she spent most of the time he was in the ring buried behind her programme and was relieved when it was all over in round six with Henry being led to his corner because of an eye injury that was not as bad as it appeared once the bleeding had been checked.

The disastrous defeat by Patterson came four months later and for the first time Mr and Mrs Henry Cooper considered his retirement from boxing. He had been humbled, but did not feel that it was the end and, as soon as she realised that he was not ready to call it a day, she said no more and never again referred to the matter. Five more wins followed and once again he was European, British and Commonwealth heavyweight champion, although such titles meant little to Albina. Judge her surprise, therefore, when he walked in one afternoon and announced that he had given up his laurels in protest to the Board of Control's action in refusing to recognise a proposed fight between Jimmy Ellis, of America, and himself being advertised as for the vacant world crown, Ali having been stripped of his title because of his refusal to serve in the American Army.

The best part of a year went by and southpaw Jack Bodell, whom Henry had already stopped in two rounds, was installed in his place. That prompted a comeback and Cooper regained his British and Commonwealth titles with a points verdict. Nine months later he re-won the European crown with a nine-round win over Jose Urtain of Spain. So he was back at the top again, and readily accepted an offer to put all his three titles at stake against Joe Bugner, although this meant giving away 2 inches in height and reach, 26 pounds in weight, and 16 years in age. Even though he was coming close to his 37th birthday, Cooper felt there was so much expertise and experience on his side to compensate for all the physical disadvantages. At the end of fifteen tense rounds, he thought he had done enough to earn a points award. So it seemed, did the majority of the ten thousand spectators – but not Referee Harry Gibbs. Unhesitatingly he held Bugner's arm aloft and Henry went back home outrageously disgusted. When he told Albina what had happened, all she said was 'Does it matter?' She was inwardly delighted when he announced that he would never fight again.

Index